Status of Girl Child in India

Status of Girl Child in India

A. Kusuma

SERIALS PUBLICATIONS
NEW DELHI (INDIA)

First Published - 2011

ISBN: 978-81-8387-485-4

Published by

SERIALS PUBLICATIONS
4830/24, Prahlad Street, Ansari Road
Darya Ganj, New Delhi-110002 (India)
Phone : 23245225 Fax.: 91-11-23272135
E-mail: serials@sify.com

Contents

Acknowledgement *vii*
List of Abbreviations *ix*

1. Introduction 1
2. Review of Literature 23
3. Methodology 72
4. Results and Discussion 84
5. Summary and Conclusions 146

References 169
Appendix (Interview Schedule) 183
Index 195

Acknowledgement

I acknowledge with a deep sense of gratitude the tireless guidance of my Research Supervisor, **Prof. K. Surekha Rao**, Department of Social Work, Sri Padmavathi Mahila Visvavidyalayam, Tirupati. Her constant encouragement at every stage of my research deserves a special mention.

I extend my respectful thanks to **Prof. G. Sarojamma**, Vice-Chancellor, Sri Padmavathi Mahila Visvavidyalayam, Tirupati, for giving me an opportunity to do my research in this university.

I convey my gratitude to **Prof. V. Uma**, Dean, School of Social Sciences, Law & Management and Head, Department of Social Work, Sri Padmavathi Mahila Visvavidyalayam, Tirupati, for her continuous support and encouragement throughout my research work.

I express my sincere thanks to the Faculty Members **Prof. K. Muragaiah**, Chairperson, BOS, Department of Social Work, and **Dr. K. ANuradha**, Associate Professor, **Mrs. I.V. Lalitha Kumari, Mrs. P. TAvitamma** and **Mrs. G. Malli Swaramma** Assistant Professors, Department of Social Work, Sri Padmavathi Mahila Viswavidyalayam, Tirupati, for extending their moral support and for creating a congenial atmosphere which helped me to complete my work.

I sincerely thank the **Librarian** and the **Library staff** of Sri Padmavathi Mahila Viswavidyalayam, Tirupati, Sri Venkateswara University, Tirupati and staff of **Centre for Women Studies**, Sri Padmavathi Mahila Viswavidyalayam, Tirupati, for their support and co-operation for providing library services.

I convey my gratitude to **Prof. K.V. Sharma**, Department of Statistics, S.V.University, Tirupati, for his continuous support to complete my research work.

I convey my gratitude to **Prof. M.P. Sastri**, Retired Professor, Department of Statistics, S.V. University, Tirupati, for his continuous support to complete my research work.

I am highly indebted to the **Deputy Mandal Education Officer, Deputy Educational Officer**, TTD, **Municipal Educational Officer**, Tirupati, for providing me with the necessary information for my research work.

My heartfelt thanks to **Prof. M. Ubaidullah**, Head, Department of Population Studies and Social Work, **Prof. V.K. Ravindra Kumar**, Chairperson, BOS, **Dr. T. Lakshmamma**, Co-ordinator, MSW and other staff, Department of Population Studies and Social Work, Sri Venkateswara University, Tirupati, for their precious suggestions and cooperation to complete my work.

My heartfelt thanks to **Dr. K. Suneetha**, Academic Consultant, Department of Population Studies and Social Work, Sri Venkateswara University, Tirupati, for her affectionate support and valuable suggestions in my research work.

My respectable thanks to **Sri R.A. Jayantha**, Retired Reader, Department of English, Sri Venkateswara University, Tirupati, for his valuable guidance and support in my research work.

I am thankful to the **respondents** (teachers) of my study for extending their co-operation during the process of data collection.

My heartfelt thanks to my **husband, children, parents, in-laws, sister, brothers** and **other family members**, who have given me constant support and encouragement in the completion of my work.

(A. Kusuma)

List of Abbreviations

AIDS	:	Acquired Immuno Deficiency Syndrome
BSY	:	Balika Samridhi Yojana
CEDAW	:	Convention on the Elimination of All Forms of Discrimination against Women
CLPR	:	Child Labour Protection and Regulation Act
CRC	:	Convention on the Rights of the Child
CSR	:	Centre for Social Research
HIV	:	Human Immunodeficiency Virus
ICDS	:	Integrated Child Development Scheme
IMR	:	Infant Mortality Rate
KGSY	:	Kasturba Gandhi Shiksha Yojana
KSY	:	Kishori Shakti Yojana
MHFW	:	Ministry of Health and Family Welfare
NCRB	:	Nation Crime Record Bureau
NFHS	:	National Family Health Survey
NPA	:	National Plan of Education
NPAG	:	Nutritional Programme for Adolescent Girls
NPE	:	National Policy of Education
NPEW	:	National Policy for the Employment of Women
NRCW	:	National Resource Centre for Women
NSSO	:	National Sample Survey Organisation
SAARC	:	South Asian Association for Regional Cooperation
SSA	:	Sarva Siksha Abhiyan
STD	:	Sexually Transmitted Diseases
UNCRC	:	United Nations Convention on the Rights of Child
UNICEF	:	United Nations International Children Emergency Fund

1

Introduction

As per the definition of the United Nations Convention on the Rights of Child (UNCRC) the term 'child' includes all persons under the age of 18 years. This definition is accepted and ratified by 192 states in the world to promote child protection and child rights. In general girl child means "a female child, from birth to the age of puberty". The census of India defines persons below the age of 14 as children. While making use of standard demographic data, "social scientists include females in the age group of fifteen to nineteen years under the category of the girl child" (education.nic.). Several government programmes for children are targeted for the age group below 14 years.

Status of the Girl Child

The girl child in most parts of the South Asian Region is born and raised in cultures which associate negative value with her as an entity. This can be attributed to age-old norms and customs related to patriarchy, religious beliefs, taboos and ethnic practices. According to Sharma (1995) there are variations in the status of the girl child across the countries, but overall, deprivation is either expressed or hidden behind 'equal status syndrome' more or less throughout the SAARC region. The hazards the girl child is exposed to seem to be endless. According to the Eleventh Five Year Plan (2007-2012) the life threatening problems of a girl child are the following (Table 1).

Table 1

Years	*Problems Faced*
Before birth to 1 year	(a) Foeticide and infanticide
	(b) Infant mortality
	(c) Discrimination in breast feeding and infant food.
	(d) Neglect of health (immunization)
1 to 11 years (this includes specific problems faced by age groups 1-5 years and 6-11 years)	(a) Discrimination in access to food and health care.
	(b) Malnutrition and anemia
	(c) Health problems like Polio and diarrhea
	(d) Iodine and Vitamin A and Micro nutrient deficiency
	(e) Low school enrollment and school dropouts
	(f) Vulnerable to trafficking, child labour, child marriage
	(g) Abuse, exploitation and violence
	(h) Domestic chores
	(i) Looking after siblings
	(j) Restriction on mobility and play
	(k) Discrimination in overall treatment and parental care.
11 to 18 years (Adolescents)	(a) Poor health
	(b) Low literacy level
	(c) Restriction on mobility and play
	(d) Frequent illness due to malnutrition, anaemia and micro-nutrient deficiency
	(e) Child marriage
	(f) Early child bearing morbidity and mortality
	(g) Poor access/denial to information and services
	(h) Early and frequent pregnancy coupled with abortions.
	(i) Marital and domestic violence
	(j) Dowry harassment, desertion, polygamy, divorce
	(k) Child labour trafficking
	(l) STDs and HIV/AIDS
	(m) Heavy domestic work including commuting long distances to collect fire wood/drinking water.
	(n) Unpaid and unrecognized work, and drudgery
	(o) No voice either in home or society.

Source : 11th Five Year Plan (2007-2012).

A male dominating society continues even today in many parts of the world. What is worse, the male child is taken as an asset to the family whereas the girl child is a considered a liability for the parents. She is considered as an outsider for all practical purposes and after marriage, she is not accepted as a true member of the husband's family also. This worsens her position, prestige and status in society. The parents of a girl child feel that once she is married off, she would be in no way helpful to them in later life. This creates a preference and longing for a male child. Along with this there are other beliefs, customs and rituals continuing for centuries which dictate that only a son is entitled to light the funeral pyre of the parents after their death and thus show the way to salvation (Mukti). "The parents who have no son, are called 'Aputraka' and given a low status in the society and feel cursed. The male child is counted as 'Swogotri' and can lead the light of continuity of his line whereas the daughter becomes 'paragotri' on marriage and is no way useful ritually for her parents in almost all activities" (Mohanty, 2005).

Thus every parent has a special inclination towards a male child. Parents have to nourish bring up and educate the girl child only to give her away in marriage. And they have to search the additional responsibilitics for the right man for her to give her away in marriage. The traditional practice of 'Stree Dhan' (give something as gift to their beloved daughter voluntarily at the time of marriage) has degenerated into a commercial transaction now-a-days in the name of 'dowry'. Dowry has become an inviolable custom and convention. It is only natural that women feel discriminated and unjustly treated. To relieve themselves of the burden of a girl child, many parents are seen neglecting the female child and if at all a girl child is born, they do not hesitate to finish her forever.

There is also a social stigma attached to the girl child. Her attaining puberty in the father's house is regarded as a sin and curse for her parents' family. This blind belief encourages child marriage because the child is married off before she attain puberty. "Though it is prohibited in law, many child marriages are taking place" (Centre for Social Research, 2007). In our society, a woman has no real independence of her own. According to Manu, she has no voice, no decision to be counted for. She is to be guided and guarded by three different persons i.e., father, husband son, and so called as 'abala' (Bhargava, 1989).

The widespread discrimination of the girl child and the gender bias affect her socio-economic status and demographic status. The girl child discrimination in India is evident from several social indicators. This is due to unfavourable attitudes prevailing in society, where the birth of a daughter is not celebrated in the same manner as the birth of a son. "Born into indifference and reared on neglect, the girl child is caught in a web of cultural practices and prejudices that hamper her development, both physically and mentally. In India, for a girl child the period from infancy to adolescence is a perilous path" (NRCW, 2003). Gender discrimination replicates itself from generation to generation, violates the rights of the girl child and choke her further development, inflict poverty and crushes her sense of autonomy. Persisting gender inequalities, existing cultural beliefs and practices permeate into almost every aspect of the growing girl's life and they are present in every society irrespective of class, caste and economic conditions. "Inspite of all the efforts made, an insight into girl child, profile indicates negative sex ratio, higher female child mortality rate, lesser access to food, health, and care" (NRCW, Gender Discrimination, 2003).

Demographic Concepts of Girl Child

Demographic characteristics of the girl child are very important in understanding her status. Demographic characteristics like sex ratio, girl child mortality, rate of child marriages, literacy levels, school enrollments and dropouts, girl child labour, etc., are clear evidences for the girl child status. According to the 2001 Census, the child population (0-14 years) was 36.14 crores. Among them 18.88 crores were males, 17.20 crore were females. The girls in the age group of 0-9 years were 11.49 crores whereas 5-7 crores were in the age group of 10-14 years. In Andhra Pradesh, the child population (0-14 years) was 2.42 crores. Among them 1.29 crores were males 1.18 crores were females. Further, the girls in the age group of 0-9 years were 7.6 million and 4% million girls were in the age group of 10-14 years.

Literacy Levels among Girl Child

Literacy for girls is a crucial input for developing human resources, which in the ultimate analysis is a national asset.

Literacy for girls has very far-reaching implications for society as well as the recipient girl. According to the 2001 census, 7.8 crore girls are literates as against 8.4 crores boys in the age group of 5-11 years and 9.5 crores girls are literates as against 10.5 crores boys in age group of 11 to 14 years. In Andhra Pradesh, 53 thousand girls are out of school in the age group of 6-11 years and 83 thousand girls who are in the age group of 11-14 years are out of school as on 31.3.2007 (www.developnation.org). On the whole 1.26% girls are out of school as against 1.15% of boys in the age group of 6-11 years and 4.42% of the girls are out of school as against 3.68% of boys in the age group of 11-14 years. The net primary enrollment ratio in 2001-2002 was 83.7%, and the children reaching grade 5 in 2000-2001 was 59.8% which show the dropout rate is rather high. Dropout rates increased alarmingly in classes from III to V. It was 50% for boys and 58% for girls. All these indicate illiteracy among children particularly among girls. 53% of girls in the age group of 5 to 9 years are illiterate (www.smilefoundation.india.org, 2003).

The mid-term appraisal of the Tenth Plan expressed concern with regard to the adverse child sex ratio, the rising incidence of female foeticide and infanticide, persistently high infant child and maternal mortality rates, wide gender gaps in child health and education as well as low female literacy and escalating violence against girls/women, etc.

According Chatterjee (2006) one of the prime reasons for the negligence of the girl child is dismal investment in resources and failure to check the imbalances in the male and female sex ratio. The patriarchal mindsets in combination with socio-religious, customary laws and traditions have further compounded the problem of the girl child by the dowry system still largely intact. As a result, having a female child is viewed as an unfeasible investment. This pernicious practice robs daughters of India not only of their right to healthy environment, good nutrition and education and the opportunity to reach their full potential, but also most basically of their right to birth.

Child Sex Ratio

The sharp decline in female sex ratios over the years suggests that female foeticide and infanticide may be primarily responsible for this phenomenon followed by the general neglect of the girl child. The sex ratio according to the 2001 census among 0-6 years was 933 in 2001 against 927 in 1991. The child sex ratio in Andhra Pradesh was 964. The sex ratio has been dwindling even in states like Haryana (820), Punjab (793), Uttar Pradesh (916) and Gujarat (878) which are supposed to be economically prosperous.

Girl Child Mortality

Female infanticide has been reported from parts of Rajasthan, Bihar, Uttar Pradesh, West Bengal and Tamil Nadu. The magnitude of girl child mortality is reflected from the fact that while every year, about 12 million girls are born in India, a third of them die in the first year of their life; three million, or 25 per cent do not survive to see their fifteenth birthday. The child mortality rate between 0-4 years for the girl child is 20.6 per cent which is two per cent more than that of the boys i.e., 18.6 per cent (Ministry of Health and Family Welfare, 2003).

Child Marriages

Child marriages still continue despite the fact that the Child Marriage Restraint Act was enacted way back in 1929. Rajasthan, Madhya Pradesh, Andhra Pradesh, Bihar and Uttar Pradesh have high incidence of child marriages.

According to the 2001 census, the number of children married in the age group of 10-14 years was 2 millions, and among them 0.6 million male children were married as against 1.4 million girl children. It clearly shows that child marriages are much more in girls than boys. In Andhra Pradesh, the children ever married in the age group of 10-14 years were 94 thousand. Among them 21 thousand were males as against 73 thousand females. There is every need to create awareness among people about the deplorable consequences of child marriages and to plug the loop holes in the law against Child Marriages.

Regarding widowhood (being deprived of the spouse); among children who were married, the total number of children widowed in India was 1 lack of them 28 thousands were males and 79 thousands were females. In Andhra Pradesh, the number of children widowed in the age group of 10-14 years was 5.4 thousand among them 1.23 thousand were males and 4.17 thousand were females.

According to the UNICEF, 82 per cent of girls in Rajasthan are married before they are 18 years, while in India 52 per cent of girls have their first pregnancy between 15 to 19 years, which leads to many undesirable consequences. For instance, their education is sacrificed for marriage which makes them totally dependent on the family and vulnerable to domestic violence etc.

Child labour flourishes in India even though there is a high level of adult unemployment, because it is the cheapest labour and easily available. Quality of education is a human right, yet more than 130 million primary school age children in the developing countries are out of schools. Nearly 60% of them are girls, as they are obliged to attend to household chores and get employed in the informal sector for supporting parental income. The 2001 census estimates child workers in crores. The Ministry of Labour puts the child workers force at 14 million, but non-government organizations insist that the figure has already crossed the mark of 100 million (Pasayat, 2000). The girl child is the mother's substitute in the family all over the country. Her work participation starts even when she is 3-4 years old, with assisting her mother in household works like collecting fuel, looking after the house and younger siblings in her mother's absence. Her real vocational training starts at the age of 8-9 years under the guidance of her mother (Mishra, 2000).

Government and Non-government organizations have failed to rescue child labourers and bring them into the mainstream. The majority of child labourers are girls and severely exploited by their employers (UNICEF, 1990). Lack of education, growing population and poverty, lack of opportunities pull the girl child into the quagmire of child labour. A significant number of girl child labourers are found in the unorganized, informal and unregulated sectors of the economy. A major portion of girl child labourers are found in the unorganized sectors and most of them are working as domestic servants. Girls representing almost half of the nation's children under the age of 18 are kept away from education, underfed, under-nourished and discriminated against, in contrast to their male counterparts in every field (Mishra, 2000).

Educational Status of Girl Child

The notion of equality of opportunity in education, as one of the prime constituents of human rights, is accepted by all civilized societies. But the one group that has yet to gain meaningful access to education are girl children in India.

Enrolling a girl child in school is a difficult job especially in rural areas, since parental resistance is comparatively high. The reasons for parental resistance are : girls are more helpful to parents in household and agricultural work than boys, education, it is felt, is not important for girls; girls have to be married off even as children; etc.

Poverty alone cannot be attributed as the cause for low literacy among girls. A number of other factors are just as responsible. According to Khan (2004) some of the conditions that lead to illiteracy are inadequate school facilities, lack of qualified female teachers, transport facilities and hostel facilities for girls, fear of sexual harassment, eve teasing, fixed schooling hours, etc. These and other create an unattractive environment for girls to remain in schools. It is not surprising that girls dropout from school in large numbers.

Education leads to human resource development comprising better health, nutrition, improved socio-economic opportunities and more congenial and beneficial natural environment for all. According to the National Sample Survey Organisation (1997), the proportion of female children in the age group of 5-14 years attending school during 1993-94 was 55.4 per cent female children as against 70.3 per cent of male children in rural areas and in urban areas, 80 per cent female children as against 84.5 per cent male children attending school.

It shows that the participation of girls even at the primary education level has been found to be unequal compared with boys of the same age. The dropping out of girls becomes more marked at the upper primary and secondary levels, which was clearly evident in the 2001 census which showed female literacy rate as 53.7 per cent as against 75.3 per cent of males literacy rate. According to Mukherjee (1991) the other reasons for low enrollment and high dropping out of girls and their low level of education of girls and their low level of education are "direct cost involved in education, opportunistic cost in the form of loss of domestic work, co-education schools". Further, education exposes girls to new ideas, which may influence their submissive role in the family.

The World Bank Report (1996) on India's primary education, stated that, the enrollment of girls increased by 20 per cent, but 15 to 20 per cent were irregular to school and 35 per cent dropped out before completing primary education. There are significant rural-urban disparities in female literacy. A striking finding is that for every 100 girls in Class I in rural areas, there are only 40 in Class-V, 18 in Class-VIII, 9 in Class-IX only one in Class-XII. The corresponding figures for urban areas are 82, 62, 32 and 14 (Convention on the Rights of the Child, 1997). Similarly, the proportion of women and girls in courses of technical education like engineering, medicine, agriculture, etc., is woefully low.

All children, both boys and girls, have a right to education till the age of 14. But studies of the girl child reveal that the girl child is made to stay at home to help the mother in domestic work and thus, denied the right to attend school and receive the facilities provided for girl child's education by the government such as free education, scholarships, etc. Though education is a human right, yet more than 130 million primary age children in the developing countries are out of schools. Nearly 60 per cent of them are girls (UNICEF Report, 2004). As noted already, domestic obligations and household chores, and getting engaged in the informal sector as servant maids for supporting their parental income are among the main causes for it.

According to the 7th All India Education Survey (2002), 53 per cent of girls in the age group of 5 to 9 years are illiterate. In India, only 53 per cent habitations have a primary schools and in nearly 60 per cent schools, there are less than two teachers to teach Classes I to V. Further, the survey reveals that high cost of private education, the girl child's need to work to support their families and little interest in studies are the reasons given why three in every four drop out of the school. And the dropout rate is increasing alarmingly at the primary level itself (58 per cent among girls) (www. smilef oun dation india.org, 2003).

Children are the supremely important asset of a nation and the nation's future lies in their proper development. A healthy and educated 'girl child' today is an active and 'intelligent citizen' of tomorrow.

Health Status of Girl Child

Growth and physical development of infants and children are widely used as indicators of the overall health and nutritional status of any community. The beliefs that culturally determine social behaviour place the female child nutritionally disadvantage. The National Family Health Survey-II (1998-1999) observed that gender disparities and differentials in nutritional intake had narrowed down. The report further revealed that median duration of breastfeeding for male child was 26.4 months whereas it was 24.6 months for the female child". Gender differential exists in nutritional status between the male and female child in the lower stratum of society based on socio-economic background of the family.

The National Institute of Nutrition study (2003) found that the prevalence of anaemia was 69 per cent among 12-14 years old adolescent girls. During the period of adolescence, the girl child faces most of the health problems, particularly those concerning reproductive health, combination of early childhood discrimination in food, nutrition, health care, neglect in adolescent girls and teenage pregnancy and poor health care services, all these affect the health status of the girl child (NRCW, 2003). The statistics on girl child shows that one out of every six girls does not live to see her 15th birth day, and every sixth girl child's death is due to gender discrimination. More than 50% of India's children are malnourished. While one in every five adolescent boys is malnourished, against one in every two girls is under nourished".

Left-over food is consumed generally by women in the family. In most of the families, it is consumed by either mother or the girls or all together. The left-over food most of the time does not have any nutrients and it is not good for health. During her adolescent age, the girl child requires extra nutritious food. Women's Studies and Development Centre's (2007) study of awareness among rural and urban mothers about girl's extra nutritive need, reveal that "only 50 per cent of mothers are aware about girl's extra nutritional needs". This indicates a lack of health education and awareness of nutritive needs of girl children among mothers. Discrimination in the provision of adequate and timely nutrition and health inputs to the girl child is a persisting problem as a result of which these groups suffer from various problems like under weight, malnutrition, anaemia, micro-nutrient deficiencies, stunted growth, etc.

Health and nutrition awareness and education to reduce discrimination against girls is essential. "An intensive social mobilization of communities especially women's group and adolescent groups needs to be undertaken and should focus on immunization of the girl child, promotion of breastfeeding, micro-nutrient deficiencies and malnutrition by removal of food taboos for girls along with regular health checkup at primary health centres" (Girl child in the Eleventh Five Year Plan, 2007-2012). Special attention should be given to more vulnerable girls especially those affected by HIV/AIDS, trafficked victims, physically and mentally challenged girls to provide them with special health and nutrition inputs.

Problems of the Girl Child in India

Children are normally dependent upon adults, particularly on parents, for their personal, emotional and material needs as well as socialization. The dependence of a girl child on adults is greater than that of a boy. It is expected that parents, guardians and the society create an adequate environment for the normal physical, mental, emotional and intellectual maturity of a girl child. "The girl child is considered to be a lesser child in our society. She continues to be neglected at all levels and discrimination against her is rampant in all strata of the society irrespective of class, caste and economic conditions" (Tripathy and Chaudhury, 2005). The existing profile of the girl child indicates a declining sex ratio, low nutritional status, high female mortality rate and school dropouts among girls.

Female Foeticide

Female foeticide is a practice of selective elimination of the female foetus after prenatal sex determination or sex pre-selection, thus avoiding the birth of a girl child. Sex determination of the unborn child is banned under Pre-natal Diagnostic Techniques Act, 1994. Moreover, utilization of ultra-sonography, amniocentesis to determine and communicate the sex of the unborn is punishable under the law since January, 1996. As technology advances and changes the mode of getting rid of a girl child also likewise changes. Female infanticide has taken the form of female foeticide. Female foeticide is fast emerging as a problem that affects all parts of the country.

The districts with the highest prevalence of female foeticide in India are Fatehgarh Sahib-747, Patiyala-764, Punjab, Salem in Tamil Nadu-763, Kureshetra and Ambala-772 in Haryana with a low child sex ratio. Contrary to the general belief that foeticide occurs where people are poor, illiterate and ignorant, the highest ratio of foeticide have been observed in economically developed areas like Punjab and Haryana (Ranjana Kumari, 2006). The causes behind female foeticide are social, economic, political and technologically-related. Foeticide as one of reproductive choices and "advertisements like spend Rs. 500 now and save Rs. 5,00,000 later" become a part of this inhuman practice, and make it sound like an economic investment" (Sorta, Bilajac, 2004). Often mothers who suffer discrimination in their entire lives do not wish to pass this legacy on to their daughters, which increasing pre-natal elimination, together with persistent, post natal risk (Sudha and Rajan, 2003).

Female foeticide is not a medical issue. It is basically a social issue and a crime. Therefore, efforts should be made from all sides and by all concerned to present this inhuman crime. Atrocities against the girl child start even before she is born, and parents themselves with the help of sex determination tests, indulge in their crime. Every year about 12 million girls are born in our country. Of them 25 per cent do not survive upto the age of 15 and the death of every sixth child is due to gender discrimination (www.smilefoundationindia.com). Census reports of 2001 clearly show that there is a significant decline in the sex ratio in 0-6 years age group, which is an indicator of accelerated disequilibrium. For this disturbing trend there are many reasons, social, economic and political which need both public and government attention and concerted action from them, both preventive and punitive.

Female Infanticide

The Infant Mortality Rate (IMR) of the girl child is higher than that of the male child. It clearly indicates the intentional neglect of and discrimination against the girl child with regard to food, nutrition and health care. Infanticide, also referred to as 'Fetal enthanasia', is the killing of a dependent innocent entrusted to the care of one who kills. Infanticide is an overtly barbaric practice, carried on by non-professional and less powerful persons e.g., traditional dai's or old ladies in the household" (Chaudhury and Tripathy, 2005).

Female infanticide is the result of parents' discouraging the life chances of unwanted daughters through selective neglect and infanticide. "Around 60 million girls reported as missing are a result of infanticide, sex, selective abortions, and neglect" (Kaur, 2006). Among the reasons for female infanticide are the desires to avoid giving dowry which is a widely prevalent menace, and get rid of unwanted new born girls. Whatever the plausible motives and reason be for female infanticide, it is a crime against humanity.

CRIMES AGAINST CHILDREN (GIRLS)

Girl child abuse or exploitation is the physical, emotional or sexual maltreatment or neglect of children by parents, guardians or by others. According to the Nation Crime Record Bureau (2006-2007), the number of cases registered under Human Trafficking during was 5,096. Of them, 35 were for buying of girls for prostitution all over India, 123 for selling girls for prostitution, 231 for procuring minor girls, 67 for importation of girls, 4,541 under Immoral Trafficking Prevention Act, 1956, and 29 under Child Marriage Restraint Act, 1929. When compared with cases registered in 2005, an increase of 59.3 per cent in procuring minor girls, 14.5 per cent for selling of girls for prostitution, and 25 per cent for buying girls for prostitution. In Andhra Pradesh, the total number of cases registered under Human Trafficking during 2006 was 720 which is 3rd highest, after Tamil Nadu-1739 and Karnataka-794.

A total of 18,967 cases on crimes against children were reported in the country during 2006 as compared to 14,975 cases during 2005, suggesting an increase of 26.7 per cent. Among the IPC crimes, the number of foeticide cases increased from 86 in 2005 to 125 in 2006, registering an increase of 45.3 per cent over 2005. A total of 126 infanticide cases were reported in the country during 2006 as against 108 in the year 2005, registering an increase of 16.7 per cent. Cases of abetment to suicide increased by 4.7 per cent during the year 2006 (43 to 45 cases).

A total of 4,721 cases of child rape were reported in the country during 2006 as compared to 4,026 in 2005 accounting for a significant increase of 17.3 per cent during the year. Madhya Pradesh has reported the highest number of cases (829) followed by Maharashtra (655). "Offenders were known to the victims in a majority (75.1%) of cases" (NCRB, 2006-2007). The conviction rate at the national level for these crimes stood at 35.4 per cent, for infanticide cases 45.5 per cent and for murder cases 43.3 per cent. "Legislatures have increased prison terms and other penalties for child sex offences who victimize multiple children or who stand in a position of trust with respect to their victims, such as guardian, parent or teachers" (www.balika.org). Andhra Pradesh reported a majority 86.2 per cent of cases (1,347) of conviction under Indecent Representation of Women (P) Act, to total cases reported (1,562) under the act in the country.

Manmeet Kaur (2006) states that annually 40 million children by the age of 14 are reported to be victims of child abuse and neglect. Girls account for about 80 per cent of the reported cases of the victims of violence and abuse. Girls are more likely to be abused by male family members.

Sexual Abuse

Girl children are increasingly victims of abuse and torture including sexual abuse. "There are numerous instances of girl child being abused by relatives, trustworthy neighbours or friends of girls' siblings" (www.savethechildren.com). According to a survey conducted by the Torture Prevention Centre of India in schools found that 44 per cent of girls experienced mental torture including eve teasing at public places, invitation to see porn magazines and indecent exposure (The Hindu, 2001).

The child prostitution is on the rise in India. 5.3 lakhs children are prostituted before they are 15 years old (Bishogi, 2003). The fear of HIV/AIDS virus has resulted in a huge demand for uninfected by children prostitute seeker. The UNICEF report on child prostitution in India confirms this by stating that "family members of girls are acting in trafficking operations. Nearly two million children are abused and forced into prostitution every year in India (My Name is Today, 2002).

According to a survey conducted by the National Commission for Women in 1997 in Andhra Pradesh, it was found that 77 per cent of the prostitutes were illiterate and 70 per cent of them had children. Most of the children lived at their place of work. If the prostitute children isolated from the mainstream and deprived of a normal life, they are denied equal opportunities. Early exposure to undesirable influences in the environment makes them highly vulnerable, which leads to the girls become prostitutes, the boys take to pimping and other antisocial activities.

Girl prostitution is practiced in all areas including the metropolitan cities of the country, though there may be variation in the forms of prostitution or modes of their operation. Girl prostitutes can be divided into different groups such as prostitutes, singing and dancing girls, religious prostitutes, those in caste-based brothels. In India, 60-70 per cent of girls are involved in prostitution because of their low socio-economic position.

Most girl child workers experience sexual harassment at their work places. The World Summit for Children (1990) adopted a convention on the rights of the child. "Article 34 of the Convention calls upon all countries to prevent the inducement or coercion of a child engaged in any unlawful sexual activity, pornographic performances and materials, the exploitative use of children in prostitution or other illegal sexual practices". ILO estimates that India has more than 4 lack child prostitutes below 15 years of age. It is contended that increasing poverty has left the young girls more vulnerable ever before. According to National Commission of Women (2003) "sixty per cent of commercial sex workers in G.B. Road, New Delhi are children". This alarming sexual exploitation of children is an important aspect of violation of human rights of girl children.

The law enforcing mechanism should consider the phenomena of child prostitution as a socio-legal and human problem and accordingly take steps under the existing legislations. Since prostitutes largely come from rural and slum areas, efforts to limit prostitution should be linked with proper development programmes of rural areas and slums.

Girl-Child Labour Force

The incidence of child labour is increasing not only in terms not only of absolute numbers, but its proportion to the total work force. Though the official figures underestimate the magnitude of the problem, the existing number of girl-child workers are much more. The unorganized labour force covers a major portion of child workers. Among the unorganized labourers, girl child workers are in a significant ratio, and are engaged in plantation, bidi/cigar rolling, match and fire works, cashew processing units, dishwashing, domestic works and as helpers in hotels, canteens and construction, sites, hawkers, etc.

Child workers, especially the girl child are pushed into the unorganized sector, because this sector has not been brought under strict restrictions of protective and prohibitive regulations, so far as the work of children are concerned. Ironically, the exploitation of girl child labour is perpetuated by the direct involvement of those very persons who are supposed to check this exploitation such as law enforcing agencies, inspection officers, parents, etc. "Nevertheless, the time has come to review all the legislations on employment of children including agricultural and domestic work where girl children are largely engaged" (Pasayat, 2005).

Cause of Girl Child Labour

Socio-economic factors are primarily responsible for the perpetuation of girl child labour. In the developing countries widespread and chronic poverty forces parents to send their girl children for work. Casteism, gender discrimination, large family size, low level of income, geographically disadvantaged area, illiteracy, etc., do contribute significantly to the girl child labour practice. Further, employers prefer girl child labour because they can be paid low remunerations; they are not unionized and therefore cannot make financial demand for overtime; they can easily managed, moulded and punished etc. In most underdeveloped and agrarian societies girl children are part of the labour force. With the growth of industrialization, they are moving from families to factories. A significant number of girl child labourers are found in the unorganized informal and unregulated sectors of the economy and a major portion of them work as domestic servants. According to Mohanty (2003) "Out of 80 million child labourers, around 60 per cent are girl child labourers". Every country rich or poor, developed or developing, technologically advanced or not, endeavours to eliminate or reduce the plight of girl child labour as none of them have right to spoil or ignore the future of girl child.

SERVICES FOR THE GIRL CHILD

Legal Support and Welfare Support for Girl Child

The girl child of today is the young woman of tomorrow. In order to develop her full potential for skills, ideas and energy, an enabling environment is required, where her intellectual, material and spiritual needs for survival, protection and development are met and her rights are safeguarded. About 42 per cent of the total population of our country are children and nearly 50 per cent of them are girls. Their basic rights for survival, development, protection and education are denied in India, which is clearly evident from the declining child sex ratio increasing female infanticides, poor educational status and national crime records.

The Central and State Governments have been aware of the problem affecting women and girl children. A number of welfare programmes have been initiated by them to enhance the status of the girl child and her survival. Further, these programmes are aimed at prevention of female foeticide, infanticide, promotion of health and nutrition, enabling education for the girl child, gender sensitization, abolition of child marriages, prevention of girl child abuse, exploitation and violence, and also to provide welfare and development services for girls.

The Indian Constitution safeguards the interests of the girl child. Article 15, Article 21, Article 24, Article 39(C), Article 39(f) and Article 45 of the Constitution are intended to protect the interest of children in general and the girl child in particular.

The UN Convention on Elimination of all forms of discrimination against women and girls was adopted in 1979. Almost hundred nations including India agreed to abide by its practice. These efforts for the advancement of women have resulted in several declarations and conventions in favour of women and girls. Moreover, in recent years, there has been a upsurge of health, nutrition and social problem if the girl child in India. The following are the various measures legal and practical by the Government of India in this regard:

1. The Dowry Prohibition Act, 1961 was launched to prohibit the giving and taking of dowry;
2. The Department of Women and Child Development has launched Integrated Child Development Scheme (ICDS) in the year 1975. Under health service components through ICDS for adolescent girls in the 11-18 years age group;
3. The Child Marriage Restraint (Amendment) Act, 1978 makes it a cognizable offence for a boy to marry before he completes 21 years and for girl before the age of 18 years;
4. In order to improve the working conditions of child labour the Government of India passed Child Labour Protection and Regulation Act, 1986;
5. National Policy of Education, 1986, proposed non-formal programmes for the child labour released from hazardous industries;
6. National Plan of Action for Girl Child for survival Protection, development and participation of girl child was prepared in the year 1991. It is recommended alternative or innovative types of special schools, taking into account their special situation should be opened exclusively for girl child labourers;
7. For prevention of female foeticide and infanticide a new scheme of 'Cradle Body' or 'Palna Scheme' was started in India, it has started first in the year 1992, Tamil Nadu state to ensure unwanted female children to be born.
8. The prenatal diagnostic techniques (Prevention of Misuses) Act, 1994;
9. 'Apni Beti Apna Desh' programmes has been introduced in 1995 to protect the girl children from work and diverting them to special schools which provide non-formal education and vocational training, supplementary nutrition and stipends;
10. In 1996, draft National Policy for the Employment of Women, (includes a section on the girl child);
11. The Balika Samridhi Yojana launched in August, 1997. Girls born after 15th August, 1997 are given a scholarship of Rs.500 per annum for 18 years if they continue in school and do not marry before the age of 18 years;

12. The Kasturba Gandhi Shiksha Yojana was announced in August, 1997 to provide state subsidies for the education of girls;
13. Immoral Trafficking Prevention Act was launched in 1998 to provide for greater penalties for the exploiters and for discriminating the sex workers;
14. Kishori Shakti Yojana (2000) launched in the year 2000 adolescent girls scheme aims to empower school dropout girls age 11-18 years through the ICDS infrastructure. It provides them education, nutrition and health related information, opportunity for self-development, skills formation and recreation. To reduce the incidence of anaemia among women and girls in particular, the Ministry of Health and Family Welfare has undertaken the prophylaxis programme to combat iron deficiency anemia by distributing iron and folic acid tablets;
15. The Sarva Siksha Abhiyan (SSA) programme of the Department of Education launched in the year 2002 aims to bring all children 6-14 years into the ambit of education for a minimum of 10 years. The SSA has a special focus on girl education and children with special needs;
16. Special nutrition package for adolescent girls is required as their health standards are very poor. Nutritional Programme for Adolescent Girls (NPAG) was started on a pilot basis in the year 2002-03 in 51 districts of the country. Under this programme, undernourished adolescent girls (body weight loss than 35 kgs) are give 6 kg of food grains per month, free of cost for an initial period of three months, if their nutritional status does not improve, they are referred to a doctor, mean while the provision of free food grains is continued.

Not withstanding these well-meant measures, the lot of girl children in particular has not improved much. According to a recent study on child abuse conducted by Ministry of Women and Child Development, Government of India, Save the Children and UNICEF (2005) 11 million children are on the streets in India without adequate parental support, 2 out of 3 children are physically abused, 53.2% children reported having faced one or more forms of sexual abuse. Further, the survey reveals that incest is the most common form of sexual abuse in homes and one child below 16 years is raped every 155th minute. More need not be said to show that the predicament of the girl child in India at present is grim.

Importance of the Study

The nation cannot afford to ignore the needs of the girl child any further, discriminate against her or just relegate her existence to the stereotyped role of a wife, mother or sister. To disregard her longer would be at the nation's peril. She needs to be recognized as the 'woman of the future' and a productive citizen of the country entitled to all the fruits of social and economic progress on an equal footing with her male counterparts. It is time, the government through various welfare programmes has been working for the welfare of the girl child. But a great deal more needs to done. At the same, the welfare of children especially girls depends very much on the opinion or attitudes of the parents towards them, which are influenced by so many socio-economic and demographic factors. "There is no dearth of literature on the girl child in India. But most of the studies deal with problems encountered by the girl child in general" (Mishra, 2000). The present study highlights the opinion of the respondents that is teachers about their girl children, as the parents' opinions are crucial. As the National Policy on Education (1986) emphasized that education needs to be used as an agent of basic change in the status of the girls and women. The teacher place a significant role in bringing attitudinal change in the society in favour of girl child. The teacher should be a model for the student. According Gafoor (2008), "the prime concern in the teaching-learning process is the teacher whose life attitudes and outlook make an impression on the students". Hence, the present study of "Parents opinion towards Girl Child – A Study amongst School Teachers in Tirupati" was planned with the following objectives:

1. To understand the socio-demographic and economic profile of the respondents (teachers);

2. To study the respondent's opinion about their girl child's education;
3. To know the respondent's opinion about their girl child's health and nutritional care;
4. To understand the respondent's opinion about their girl child's social participation;
5. To explore the respondent's opinion about their girl child's psychological development;
6. To study the respondent's opinion about their girl child's employment support;
7. To find out the respondent's opinion about the Government welfare schemes for the betterment of girl child;
8. To compare the respondent's opinion about their girl child's education with the type of school they are working, the training they have undergone the number of daughters they have and their income level;
9. To assess the effect of family income and family size on the respondent's opinion about their girl child's health and nutritional care;
10. To find out the impact of respondent's sex, religion, marital status, type of family on their opinion regarding their girl child's social participation;
11. To find out the effect of the respondent's sex and education, their opinion regarding their girl child's psychological development;
12. To know the effect of the type of school the respondents work, their marital status, and their opinion about their girl child's employment support;
13. To observe the influence of respondent's sex, and their income on their opinion regarding girl child welfare schemes; and
14. To identify the impact of the socio-economic aspects of the respondent on their opinion regarding girl child's education, health and nutritional care, social participation, psychological development and employment support.

2

Review of Literature

Indian society is structured in a hierarchical relationship that has its roots in socialization, prejudices, and discrimination against the girl child. Sex segregated norms are practiced among all sections of people. Girls are confined in home to do household work and are trained for future married life and child-rearing. Boys and girls are treated differently in family and society.

Millions of girls sacrifice their childhood, their health and their vital years of education in earning livelihood for the family. To provide a safe and secure environment along with proper opportunities for the growth and development of the girl child is essential. Several measure have been taken to improve the status of the girl child in India, particularly in educational, social, medical and health related fields through sustainable development. The status of the girl child is changing gradually mainly due to legislative measures, social developments, increasing educational opportunities etc., and awareness of the problems of the girl child through the media. However, a great deal remain to be done. Changes in the status of girl child require changes in the social structure, social relationship, upbringing and socialization process, her empowerment in family and reorientation of parental attitude as well.

Every social grouping in the world has specific traditional and cultural practices and beliefs. Some customs are beneficial to all the members, while others are harmful to a specific group, such as women and children. The traditional cultural practices reflect values and beliefs held by members of a community. Balingar (1999) points out that "In recent times, the low status of the girl child in India has received much attention. Press reports and studies have pointed to the prevalence of discrimination against the girl child not only by men but even by women including mothers". There is thus an urgent need to change the negative attitudes of the family, especially those of mothers, in order to ameliorate the condition of the girl child.

It is only through parents and family that a girl child obtains identity, means of survival, support and sustenance. Hence, the main thrust of the present research is to study in depth the parents' opinion about their girl child's education, health and nutritional care, social participation, psychological development, employment support and about government welfare programmes for girls.

As the following pages would show there have been several studies of the girl child in our society, and the various problems and challenges the girl child has been facing for decades. But there appear to be very few studies which specifically focus on the attitude of parents to their girl children. Further, no attempt seems to have been made to investigate the attitude of parents who are also teachers towards girl children. One who is both a parent and a teacher carries a double responsibility. Not only has he/she to bring up the children (girl or boy or both) at home but has to educate the minds and hearts of her / his pupils at school. Inevitably, the parent-teacher's understanding of the girl child's problem will have to be more sensitive and comprehensive than that of a mere parent or teacher. And hence, it may be said in all modesty that the present investigations mark a point of departure from other studies in the field.

Early marriage or child marriage is a problem which some girls face. The practice of giving away girls in marriage at the age of 11, 12, or 13 is prevalent in Asian, African countries. The main reasons of this practice is the girl's virginity and bridal price. Child marriage robs a girl for her childhood time which is necessary to develop her physically, emotionally and psychologically. This impose great emotional stress and health complication on the young girls. "Government should mobilize all educational institutions and the media to change negative attitudes and values towards the female gender and project a positive image for women in general, and the girl child in particular" (Mathew, 2000).

In the patriarchal family structure, a young woman's prestige or recognition in her husband's home is based on her fertility in general and the birth of a son in particular.

Girl Child Education

Despite the fact that education is symbolized the Goddess Saraswathi, yet women's education in India did not get any attention because of traditional bias against girls going to school. This was also due to the purdah system in some parts of the country, early marriages, poor economic conditions of the family and lack of awareness about the importance of girls' education. The literacy rate of India's at present is 65.38, with male literacy at 75.85 per cent and female literacy at 54.16 per cent which clearly shows the disparity in the educational status of girls and boys. The participation of girls even at the primary education level has been found to be unequal compared to that of boys. The dropping out of girls has become more marked at the upper primary and secondary levels.

The millennium development goals ensure development of girls by promoting gender equality. Barbara et al. (2003) say that to achieve universal primary education, millennium development goals ensure that by 2015 children will be able to complete a full course of primary schooling. To accomplish the goal and promote gender equality and empowerment, gender disparity has to be eliminated in primary and secondary education preferably by 2015 and at all levels of education with a focus set on ensuring girl's full and equal access to and achievement in basic education of good quality.

Education for girls is one of the strong needs for improvement in fertility, health and nutrition outcomes. Girl's education impacts on infant and child mortality and enhances family welfare. Barbara's et al. (2003) after their study of 63 countries conclude that gains in women's education has made the single large contribution to decline in malnutrition during 970-1995, accounting for 43 per cent of the total progress.

Education of women and girls is an important variable affecting demographic behaviour such as age at marriage, reproduction, infant and child mortality, migration and labour participation. According to Kanitkar (1988) "a very high degree of sustainable motivation is required on the part of parents to send the girls to school and retain them in school". His study carried out in Bihar, attempts examines the aspiration of parents /decision-makers in the family regarding the minimum level of education to be given to girls. The study reveals that the education aspired for the girls is invariably lower than that for the boys in rural as well as urban areas of Bihar. About 23 per cent of the respondents were of the opinion that girls should be given only the barest education i.e., to make them just literate.

Educational backwardness of women and girls has been both the cause and result of their low status and subordinate position in society (Mohsini, 1991). Education is a significant instrument for uplifting women's status and for reducing inequality among men and women. For village girls, work in their families begins at a very young age. It is quite common to see young girls carrying water from common wells, gathering fuel, cleaning house and laundry, etc. Despite substantial progress in providing equal educational opportunities over the past few decades, girl's access to education lags behind that of boys. Though enrollment of girls has increased the dropout rate at all levels is higher for girls than boys. The reasons for this are poverty, early marriage, helping parents in domestic work, indifference of parents, onset of puberty, etc.

Education as an element of social development is a key factor in alleviating the plight of the girl child. According Gangrade (1995) in India, even compulsory elementary education has remained an elusive goal for a majority of the girls from slums, rural and tribal areas. However, a study of the author demonstrates that the position of girl child is fast changing for the better because all measures of social development, like literacy and life expectancy have improved greatly. Bringing about changes in the status of the girl child requires rebuilding the entire social world.

Mukhopadhyay (1997) has compared 'girl child in three Indian states' and found that in Bihar 71.3 per cent respondents have illiterate mothers, 42.2 per cent of the respondent girls have never attended any school. Further, the study states that 66 per cent were dropouts from schools due to economic reasons, 65.2 per cent for familial reasons. 96.5 per cent girls were found engaged in household work. Further, household survey reveals that all girl children in rural households are in fact disguised child labourers, with the degree of exploitation varying with socio-economic backwardness.

Girl's schooling is ill-suited to the requirement of the village community and households in Mogra according to Patel (1998). He found, from his study that, enrolling children in school that the parents' willingness mattered more than that of the children. School for girls is considered as wasteful expenditure. But changes are observed in Mogra, the parents are sending their girl children to schools meant for 'girls only'. But attendance is very low. Parents find it difficult to provide necessary things like books, cloths, food, etc., to their children. Those who send their daughter have to sacrifice their comforts and work hard to send their daughters to school regularly and retain them there.

The existing disparities in the demographic, economic and social indicators between males and females are a consequence of gender inequality faced by the girl child. To overcome this the girl child needs equal access to education and opportunities to develop on par with boys. Sharma (2007a) in her study of "Home-based Intervention for improvement of socio-emotional competencies", carried out with the help of Indian Council of Agricultural Research, developed an intervention programme for mothers of deficient babies in rural areas the results revealed that significant improvement was observed in children in communication skills, daily living skills. Further, the study revealed that boys were at par with girls in all skills.

Sisodia in his study of "Girls Literacy in India" (2003) found that the dropping out rate of girl children was due to several causes 56 per cent due to involvement labour and agricultural work. 42 per cent due to work related to household activities, 42 per cent because of siblings, 24 per cent because of marriage etc., and 10 per cent because of eve-teasing etc. The study enquired about the girl child's opinion of education. It was revealed that 28 per cent of girl children said that girls should be educated to understand their routine work only, 25 per cent of parents felt that girls should be educated as much as possible, 17 per cent felt that girls should be educated upto they become self-dependent. Further, the study revealed that, 48 per cent of the parents are not in a position to give any suggestion for the betterment of girl child education.

In Mukherjee Saraswath (2005) a study "Women's empowerment and gender preferences for children : A study of four metropolitan cities in India" based on National Family Health Survey-2 in four metropolitan cities, Delhi, Mumbai, Calcutta and Chennai, the relationship of different measures of empowerment and the socio-cultural settings to gender and educational preferences for children are examined. The study reveals that women with exposure to the mass media, those with little age difference from husbands and those who have control over economic resources are more favourable to girls' education. Further, the study reveals that women in Calcutta who are not involved in decision-making also favour girls' education.

Pradhan et al. study (2005) regarding attitudes towards girls' education, reveals that the respondents that education is necessary for the girl child to find a good marital alliance. This enough if she is taught to read and write letters, teach her own children and to earn money by doing some job in times of financial crisis. Some of the respondents however are totally against female education. The girl child, they hold must be confined to the four walls. Girl child's education is a liability to parents because to find grooms for educated girls is difficult and expensive. So parents are reluctant to educate girls.

Though education was made a fundamental right in India in 2002, there are countries homes with thousands of children still out of school. According to Chugh (2005) among 5,546 school-age children in Sanjay Colony, a slum settlement in Delhi, who of them 1200 were enrolled in a state-provisioned primary school, 1000 children were enrolled in an unrecognized formal school run by an NGO within the habitation while 300 attended a non-formal centre run by the same NGO. The only primary school in the area had a teacher student ratio of 1 : 125. Further, it was found that the inability of parents to bear expenses on books, uniforms and stationery was a significant cause of low enrollment. Another constraint is that the only primary school in the area, is not able to cater to the needs of all children of the 6-10 years of age group. Chugh's study highlights the fact that the parents here want to educate their children, boys and girls both, but are deterred by crumbling infrastructure and want of schooling facilities at an easily accessible distance. The findings of this study actually idea reflect the situation regarding education facilities in the slum areas of various other cities and towns in India. Rapid increase in urbanization in the coming years would further complicate the situation if timely action is not initiated now itself by providing adequate social services like education, health, employment and human safety. Otherwise the situation may go beyond all correction.

India has made concerted efforts in the last four decades to realize the goal of universalization of elementary education. Despite significant improvement in the educational facilities the goal of universalisation of elementary education remains elusive because of high dropout rates both at primary and elementary levels of education. Roul and Sahoo (2005) conducted a study to identify the causes for dropping out among girls. The investigators, through survey methods collected the views of teachers and students about literary and education. It is found that home conditions like illiteracy of parents, absence of tradition of girl's education in the family, sickness in the family, inadequate time available for study due to household work, parents' want of interest in girls education, conditions like the school being at a distance from home, lack of teaching materials in school, failure in examination, lack of women teachers etc., are the causes for girls dropping out from school. Further, social conditions such as harassment of school-going girls by local unsocial elements, marriage of girls at lower age and poor economic condition of parents also contribute to the dropping out of girl-students. Most girls in Mayurbhanj district still remain out of school due to their parents' poverty and illiteracy. In India as in the developing countries, women are less likely to want to continue their education to higher levels and are more likely to be found concentrated in such occupations as teaching, nursing, social work, typing and stenography, etc.

For the full development of human resources, for the improvement of our home and for moulding the character of our children during the most impressionable years of infancy and childhood education of women is essential. Women's education is far more important than that of men in this regard (Agrawal, 2006).

Srivastava (2006) in his study states that according UGC Annual Report, 2003-2004 there are 320 universities, with 99.54 lakh students enrolled in all courses and levels. Of them 40.03 lakh are women students constituting 40.22 per cent. The constraints to women's participation in higher education are societal, like educating the girl will not bring any gain to her family as she will go away to another family after her marriage. Further the demands of dowry also decrease the chances of girl's higher education.

Motivated by the proven benefits of women's education, the Ethiopian government, like other governments in the world, has taken a series of measures to promote women's education and improvement over the past three decades. Tilaye and Bendru (2006) carried out a study to examine the level of gender disparity in mathematics performance in the second cycle of primary education in Addis Ababa, with a view to providing the basis for developing appropriate strategies. Out of the total sample of 611 students drawn from 10 schools, 302 were girls and 309 boys. Standardized mathematical test was used for data collection. The results show that 48.2 per cent of boys and

56 per cent girls showed 'low' level performance, 30.1 per cent of boys and 24.8 per cent of girls had achieved an 'average' level of performance and 16.8 per cent of boys and 8.3 per cent girls had achieved a 'high' level of performance in mathematics. The study also reveals that the students felt that boys are naturally superior to girls in mathematical ability. This implies that traditional stereotypic views pertaining to human academic performance in favour of males still have not lost their hold on the minds of school students of Addis Ababa.

According to Loya Maisham (2009) 80 million girls aged 6 to 11 years all over the world do not even go to school. According to the vital statistics cited by the United Nations of the 110 million children are not in schools, approximately 60 per cent are girls. By the age of 18, girls have received an average of 4.4 years of education which is less than boys. To overcome this situation at the International Conference on Population and Development in Cairo in 1994 it was agreed to eliminate all forms of discrimination against the girl child and the root cause of son-preference, which results in harmful and unethical practices regarding female infanticide and sex selection before birth.

Girl Child Health and Nutrition

The nutritional status depends upon access to food. It has been suggested that females are discriminated against in food allocation. The males are given priority both in quality and quantity of food served as they are the earning members of the family. Such discrimination increases in time of food shortage and the females suffer from this deprivation.

The girl child gets doubly affected being a female and a child. She gets the lowest priority when it comes to resource allocation in terms of food, health care, access to education and training, rest and leisure time activities, inheritance and so on (Desai, 1995). Unequal access to family resources affects the girl child throughout her life and she is unable to take any decision regarding her own physical needs. Thus, the root of her ill health lies in her socio-cultural and economic position in the family and society.

As far as health is concerned, girls receive significantly less response from others at home to illness in terms of hospital care and medicines. "In most hospitals male admissions form 65 per cent of all children admitted. Girls also have higher death rate from measles, diarrhoea and acute respiratory infection" (Vandana, 1997).

Prevailing social values regard males as bread-winners of the family, and therefore they should be served food first. Secondly girls are the support system of the mothers and are activity engaged in almost all the household work with their mothers, and hence it is not possible for them to eat first. Sharma et al. (1997) in their study of 'Nutritional status of girl child–a positive change' conducted in Hissar district, under the ICDS scheme found visible discrimination in the nutritional status of adolescent girls and the various factors associated with the discrimination. The results revealed that the nutritional status of the girl child is worse than that of boys of the same age and hence malnutrition and its severity is greater among girls. And most of the girls are among the last ones in the family to eat. Boys on the other hand are the first one to be served food.

Parents, specially mothers, should try to understand the problems of the their daughters and give them full guidance and security. They should try to create an atmosphere at home that will help the healthy physical and mental growth of girls. Ruiselova (1998) analyzed the occurrence of adjustment problems in relations with parents and teachers with respect to the pubertal maturation timing in 957, 15-year old adolescent girls in Solvakia and the occurrences of externalization of problems of adjustment in connection with the above. Results of the study showed a greater occurrence of the problems in early maturing girls. There was a pronounced high occurrence of these problems in combination with objectively perceived early maturation and with subjectively perceived early maturation.

Discrimination against female children in India with regard to immunization is not a major problem. According to NFHS-II (1998-99), 43 per cent boys which is slightly more than that of girls (41 per cent) were fully vaccinated. Regarding access to health care there is a disparity in availing health care services between boy and girl children. The studies carried out in Jay Prakash Narayan Hospital, reveal that malnutrition diarrhoea etc., are more common in females than males. But it was observed that while most of the males are hospitalized frequently, females are brought hospital too late, resulting in a proportionately higher rate of mortality among them.

Statistical analysis of data on girl child reveals her invisibility. Her concerns are often subsumed in the concerns of children in general. There is evidence of negative male/female ratios, higher female children mortality, lesser access to food, health, education and recreation and early induction into domestic work, marriage and motherhood. "The perpetuation of a cycle of more burden and less care for females starts at birth and continues unabashedly during the prime years of growing up as a girl, leading to an oppressed womanhood" (Karkal, 1999).

Socializing girls from their childhood onwards to accept their situation as inferior and the ideology of male supremacy assures continuance of the discriminatory treatment of girls (Karkal, 1999). Studies in two villages of Uttar Pradesh also reveal the same. It is found that discrimination started at birth, even though many mothers would not admit it right way. While there was no discrimination in the amount of cereals consumed by both boys and girls, there were marked differences with regard to milk and milk products, egg, ghee and other items.

In many homes mothers and girls are the last to eat, when at times even the basic food was not enough. Santhi Gosh (1999) observed that there was an attempt to feed the girls less in order to delay adolescence so that, the parents would have enough time to look for a groom and collect enough resources for giving dowry. Boys ate more of raw vegetables and fruits when they were out of the house and had some pocket money for school as well. Girls hardly ever went out and did not attend school and so were denied these extraportions.

The occurrence of differences of opinion between adolescent girls and their parents in some issues and their health and nutrition are very basic to the issues that involve women as it is not only directly reflective of their status in their family but also of the well-being of the family, especially that of the girl child. Archinald et al., (1999) examined the degree to which pubertal development and parent-adolescent relationships were associated with girl's current and future dieting and body image. 127 early adolescent girls (aged 10-14 years) who were predominantly of normal weight were observed for 2 consecutive years, compared measures assessing their dieting, body image and their weights and rights etc. The results indicated that girl's perceptions of their relationships with their parents were associated with their dieting attitudes and behaviour and body image at time 1 and time 2.

In any family, women generally are involved in the provision of health care of the member. Besides, women prepare meals for and feed the sick, care for the disabled at home, take care of children and their immunization and curative care. According to Geervani (2000), "it is the woman who teaches the children personal hygiene and sanitation and lays the foundation for knowledge of health" Yet, woman is not considered as an entity in her own right i.e., having proper health care.

Nair and Pejaver (2001) analysed the awareness level of adolescent girls regarding family life in Tiruvananthapuram, Kerala. It was found that 30 per cent of the girls had eye problems, 41 per cent had ENT problems and 35 per cent dental problems. Further, 82 per cent of girls were aware of menses before menarche and 67.7% had menstrual problems and pain during periods and 81.5% girls took daily bath during periods. And also their study revealed that 39% of the students hesitated to discuss their problems with their parents and their friends. It indicates that the girls are not taken into confidence and given enough scope to discuss their problems with other family members. Parents have to encourage their girl children to discuss their problems, clarity, doubts and provide correct information to them. Lack of proper information and confusion may lead adverse effects on their health.

The health of adolescent and young girls is very important. Mother is the central figure to provide child care, nutrition and even primary health care. But, the health care of adolescent girls, which requires utmost care, is mostly neglected. The adolescent girl who is taking up the burden of procreation and care of progeny, requires sound health in order to have healthy future generation. According to Kanakadurga (2003) "Malnourishment and limited access to health care are more evident among females than males from birth onwards resulting in poor height and weight in adolescent girls".

In the patriarchal family structure, a young woman's prestige or recognition of her status in her husband's home is based on her fertility in general and her giving birth to a son in particular. According to the NRCW (2003) several studies have found that almost all societies of the world have valued sons more than daughters and have shown a marked preference for male children.

Every girl child should be aware about menstruation, which is an important event at the threshold of adolescence and ideally a mother should be the main informant at that tender age. Mother has to talk to her daughter regarding its significance, the hygienic practices and healthy attitude adopted towards menstruation. In a study conducted among 664 school girls age 14-18 in Mansoura, Egypt by EL-Gilany et al. (2005) it was found that the mass media were the main source of information about menstrual hygiene, followed by mothers. The study also observed that personal hygiene among girls was generally found to be poor, such as not changing pads regularly, not bathing during menstruation because of lack of privacy and other restrictions.

Nutritional intake during the adolescence period may have long term health implications. Total nutrient needs are higher in adolescence than during any other time in the life-cycle because of rapid growth and development. Maheswari (2005) conducted a study of 69 adolescent girls, studying 8th and 9th class in government school at Hyderabad. Pre-tests and post-test were carried out to know the impact of the awareness programme on knowledge, balanced diet etc. The result of the pre-evaluation test of knowledge about balanced diet revealed that 79.71 per cent respondents were poor in that knowledge and 20.29 per cent were average. In the post-evaluation test of the knowledge about balanced diets 17.29 per cent were found to have average knowledge and 82.6 per cent good knowledge. The results revealed that the nutrition education programme, increased the knowledge of adolescent school girls.

Children are the parents' strength, resources and hope for the future. The purpose of teaching children in primary school (6-12 years age group) basic health and development concepts is to improve their knowledge and in turn that of their parents and the community. Education for health is a fundamental right of the child. Every child is entitled to good health facilitates, educational achievement, quality of life and economic productivity. Pandy and Prasad (2006) examined 'the child-to-parents communication technique' with a sample of 22 students (health education package was given) and their 44 parents purposely selected for the study. The results revealed that 90 per cent children had medium acceptance of healthy practices before the exposure to health education. After health education, 72.72 per cent showed high acceptance of healthy practices. The results further revealed that in teaching and learning process communication through children to parents is an applicable strategy. So that all children must be provided an opportunity to acquire education to improve their knowledge as well as that of their parents.

Erratic eating habits of adolescents, if unchecked, might affect their health. Intake of fast foods, irregular food habits and attempts to curtail food intake to reduce weight, appear to be constant factors related to nutritional deficiency signs in girls. Jaya and Jaya (2006) designed a study to check the feasibility of 'school as a health promoter among adolescent girls'. The study aimed at showing how schools can function to create health awareness, develop positive attitudes and inculcate healthy practices among selected adolescent girls through effective Health Promotion Programme (HPP). The study revealed that a huge majority (88 per cent) of teachers reported that after the HPP, adolescent girls gained confidence to lead a healthy life. 75 per cent developed skills in planning and organizing health activities and 75 per cent were able to communicate health messages with their peers. 86 per cent of girls expressed that they gained information which they had not known till then, which enriched their practical experiences. Further, 77 per cent of the girls felt that the health club of the HPP was a unique opportunity for them and 75 per cent expressed the view that the HPP helped them to take nutritious foods and being about a change in their behaviour. Now they are seen offering fruits on birth days, writing health messages on notice boards, consuming vegetables, etc. The study proved that health promotion at schools would enhance the Human Development Index.

Sharma (2007b), in her project on "Comprehensive Child care through farm Creche-Intervention for Optimum Developmental Outcome of Young Children" aimed to educate mothers regarding scientific child care and evaluate the impact of intervention and developmental outcomes of infants. The results indicated a heightened performance of the infants, and improvement in knowledge regarding childcare and nutritional temperament of their mothers in the experimental group. Infants of the experimental group also showed better adaptability, adjustability, less stranger anxiety and a positive mood. Intervention for mothers made the home environment stimulatory to children for enhancing motor and mental development.

Sharma (2007c) conducted a study titled "Assessment of health status of adolescent girls belonging to Gaddi tribes of Himachal Pradesh". She chose a sample of 400 from Kangra and Chamba districts. Each district ten villages were selected to get information. The study showed that the literacy rate of tribal girls was low. The height and weight of girls were comparatively less than the NCHS and ICMR standards. Adolescent Gaddi girls were suffering from moderate to severe anaemic conditions and deficiency of Vitamin A, protein, iron and calcium. The daily nutrient intake of girls in the age group of 11-17 years found to be less as compared to the recommended daily allowances.

A survey conducted by Shinde (2007) in 22 tribal villages in Maharashtra's Nandurbar district, revealed very disturbing facts about the level of malnutrition among children. The root of the problems is the absence of sustainable means of livelihood. Further, it is noticed by author that 98 tribal children died in three months of 2005. Of these, 71 children were found to be severely malnourished. Girls constituted around half of the total number of malnourished children.

During illness, fewer women than men seek and receive treatment. Verma and Verma (2007) finds that the proportion of women to men is 1 : 3 in terms of their practice of availing themselves of hospital facilities. Women have neither time, mobility, money nor leisure, and outside child care assistance, to walk to the health centres, hospitals, etc.

Adolescence according to the WHO is the period between 10 to 19 years of age. Adolescents comprise 20 per cent of the global population. Of them 85 per cent are living in the developing countries (Prakash, 2007). Swarnalatha and Vasantha (2007) made an attempt to study the socio-economic profile of adolescent girls and evaluate their beliefs and knowledge of puberty. They find that for 36 per cent the source of first information about menarche for them was their mothers, and 52 per cent attained puberty between 14-16 years Further, the study reveals that 90 per cent of the girls were restricted by their parents to go temples during the periods, 66 per cent were confined to a room, 59 per cent girls were not allowed to enter the kitchen during periods. Further, the girls felt, the ideal age for marriage for them is 18-22 years, and they preferred to have one male and female child and only 16 per cent of them were aware about family planning methods. Further, 92 per cent of girls were in favour of having prior knowledge regarding reproductive health and they preferred to about learn them through doctor (42 per cent), mother (32 per cent). The results clearly show that the sample population has poor knowledge of reproductive health. It follows that adolescent girls need proper health education.

Adolescent girls constitute a vulnerable group and neglected one. Menstruation is still regarded as something unclean or dirty in Indian society. Menstruation and menstrual practices are still clouded by taboos and socio-cultural restrictions result in adolescent girls remaining ignorant of the scientific facts and hygienic health practices which sometimes result in adverse health problems. Dasgupta and Sarkar (2008) conducted a descriptive study among 160 adolescent girls in Singur, West Bengal to know about their awareness and status of menstrual hygiene. The results revealed that 67.5 per cent were aware of menstruation prior to attainment of menarche, and mother was the first informant regarding it for 37.5 per cent girls. 48.75 per cent girls knew the use of sanitary pad and only 11.25 per cent girls used sanitary pads during menstruation. For cleaning purpose 97.5 per cent girls used both soap and water but the frequency of cleaning was unsatisfactory. Regarding restrictions, 85 per cent girls practiced different kinds of restriction during menstruation. Menstrual hygiene, a very important factor for reproductive health maintenance, is a vital aspect of health education for adolescent girls. School teachers and knowledgeable parents can play a very important role in creating awareness about menstrual hygiene to adolescent girls.

Health education is essential for achieving a healthy mind in a sound body which develops an integrated and well organized personality and imparts knowledge and information necessary. During adolescence there is vigorous growth in body and mind. Adolescent boys and girls require education and training for maintaining sound reproductive health for which according to Das, the scholar, sex education is essential. Owing to various influences and curiosity some adolescents to involve in sex which may lead to infection of various sexually transmitting infections, etc. Further, Das (2008) states that, risk of transmission of HIV/AIDS is there as about 83.99 per cent of HIV/AIDS case are transmitted through sexual relations only. So from a holistic perspective, people in general and adolescents in particular should develop a healthy mind in a sound body with well-organized and well-integrated personality to live in health and peacefully with other members of society.

Das (2008) explored in six states in the mid-Indian tribal belt, the level of child under-nutrition among scheduled tribes, in comparison with that among the scheduled castes, other backward classes and other castes. He notices that, scheduled tribe children are poorly nourished compared to others. They are stunted, under-weight compared with 'other' communities children. Das observes that poor economic condition and a host of other factors are the probable causes for undernourishment being high among the scheduled tribes. Further, the results indicate that children in scheduled tribes are at a higher risk of under-nutrition than children in both developed and backward states.

According to Loya Mainsnam (2009), in some countries of sub-Saharan Africa, adolescent girls have HIV rates which are upto five times as high as those of adolescent boys. Further, pregnancies and child-birth, reveal health problems which take the lives of nearly 1,46,000 teenage girls every year. An estimated 450 million adult women in developing countries are stunted, a direct result of malnutrition in early life.

Girl Child Discrimination

The gender discrimination against the girl child in relation to health, nutrition, education, work participation and adolescence have been discussed by Chaudhury (1995) in his study of "Girl child and Gender bias". Further, he notices rural and urban differences and indicates measures to improve the status of the girl child such as provision of legal and welfare support and to bring about change in the attitude of parents and society through awareness programmes.

Kain (1998) says that sex determination may lead to girl child elimination'. Female fetuses are eliminated through abortions. A number of sex determination clinics are established in the country where doctors offer hopes to couple to realize their cherished dream of having a son, and in the process they abort female foetuses.

The root of the problem of discriminatory treatment being meted out to girls lies in the status of women in society and their expected roles (Karkal, 1999). Girls are socialized into docility and obedience and total dependence. This condition begins at home and is reinforced by society. The educational system and the media promote the image.

In India, the birth of girl child is still not welcome, despite a decade devoted to women and a year to the girl child. Sometimes even girls are taken care of equally along with boys in their childhood. But they will be discriminated as they grow up and reach puberty in their social living and behaviour. They will be discriminated in enjoying human rights like education, recreation, decision making, etc. According to Veena Edige's (2000), study of girl children who belong to the higher socio-economic level 86 per cent of the girls are not discriminated at all, at home in school or in society. Among the sample 300, 163 girls were first born, 99 second born and the remaining 38 are third or fourth born. Further, the study it revealed that the families never made the girl child to feel unwanted at any stage of life. The study also mentions that the difference comes when girls reach puberty. The girl child is expected to be a submissive persons, give up her tomboyish ways, sit, talk and behave like a young lady. The change in the attitude of parents may lead to confusion among girls regarding their identity. They face problems in adjusting sudden changes brought in the minds of their parents and relatives regarding their behaviour. Imposing restrictions on them may cause confuse and restlessness to them regarding their situation in the family as well as in society.

In India, child labour is a violation of our constitutional commitment to social and, economic justice, equality of opportunity and dignity of the individual. Yet, many children are engaged in various occupations and processing units etc., making a mockery of the constitutional provision. Goyal (2005) says that the Ludhiana hosiery industry, which extensively uses child labour contributes about 30 per cent of total industrial production of the state. He conducted a study with 137 child labourers who are working in the hosiery industry. The study revealed that 50 per cent of the respondents belonged to families below the poverty line. In 20.44 per cent of the cases the child was the sole wage earner in the family Most of the respondents stated that they were working in a very poor working environment, which affected them physically and psychologically. 31.11 per cent of the child-workers reported that they were ill-treated by their employer. Further, the children were also exploited by their parents for short and narrow gains. The parents usually secured loans from employers and surrendered their children as security. The findings of the study suggest that there is an urgent need of strict enforcing of child labour laws for the well-being of children.

The figures released by Census, 2001 dispel the belief that poverty is responsible for gender-biased abortions, and show that in actual fact the poor treat girls better than the rich. The Census, 2001 statistics reveal that the child sex ratio between the age group of 0 to 6 years in slum areas of 26 states is 919 girls compared to 904 girls for 1000 males in "non-slum areas" inhabited by families of well-off people. According to some reports, technology, particularly pre-natal sex determination test, is responsible for lower girl child numbers in urban non-slum areas.

Child marriages continue to be a fairly well accepted social norm in India. This was in the past reinforced when Brahmanical law-givers imposed strict religious and social sanctions against marrying girls who were above 10 years of age. It is unfortunate that even after numerous reforms and laws child marriages are still rampant in different parts of the country. Leni Chaudhury (2005) says that the median age at marriage in India is the lowest in world. On an average, 38.4 per cent girls in the age group of 15-19 years (before the legal age for marriage was made 18) are married off. The mean age at marriage for girls in urban areas is 17 years while in rural areas it is 14 years. The causes for child marriages are poverty related patriarchal system and other factors to keep girls protected from problems like sexual violence, rape, incest, etc. Under these circumstances child marriages are seen as the only way to provide protection to girls, which results young girls who are married at an early age are denied opportunities for education and skill development. They grow up as adults with no special skills, rendering them unfit to join the work force. This impairs them from economic self-reliance, thus, making them vulnerable and dependent on male members of the family. Girl child marriage and mandatory sexual relations with her husband expose her to another kind of health hazards caused by early pregnancy. Further, forced sex results in vaginal tears, bleeding and shock.

Apart from foeticide, sheer neglect is killing more young girls than boys in India and China than in the rest of the world. The W.H.O. annual report on world health gives these alarming statistics that show the extent to which prejudices run against girls even after they are born. "Normally, the survival rates for girls are higher than boys and more girls are dying in under 5 age group in India (Pumphi, 2005).

Trafficking in children is `a glaring instance of the deep-rooted problems of a society that has last the ability to care for and protect children. The innocent children of socio-economically backward families are trafficked by anti-social elements and criminals. Deb (2005) states that child-trafficking has become a serious social problem in some parts of India. West Bengal is one of the badly affected states. Especially at risk are the girl children of rural areas from poor families. There is the need of preventive measures against such atrocities by improving the rural economy and creating awareness in rural areas, along with the involvement of panchayat members and local administrators as well as NGOs in this endeavour.

Though historically child marriages were in vogue in all communities, with the advent of modernity the ruling classes gradually gave up this practice. Saraswathi (2006) in her study says that poverty and rising marriage costs are the main reasons for child marriages. Further, as observed by the United Nations International Children Emergency Fund (UNICEF), the poor families may regard a young girl as an economic burden and her early marriage as survival strategy for the family. Further, the parents think that early marriage offers protection to the daughters against sexual assault. Apart from serious health consequences child marriage also takes away the educational opportunities of a girl child.

Sex ratio is an important social indicator to measure the prevailing equity between males and females in a society at a given point of time. Further, it reflects the underlying socio-economic and cultural pattern of a society in different ways. Nagda (2006) explains that the reason for low child sex ratio is discrimination against the girl child by the family as against the boy child considered the future bread-winner of the family. Having more male children is considered as enhancing one's status. Further the evil practice of dowry also contributes to the low child sex ratio.

Trafficking is integrally linked to the lack of secure livelihood. Resultant insecurity forces large numbers of people to leave their homes, go to other places seeking income to improve their living conditions. According to Chowdury (2006) the incidence of trafficking in women and girl children over the past decade has escalated considerably. Further, the bulk of trafficking in the South Asian Region, both trans-border and in country, happens for the purpose of commercial sexual exploitation, and 60 per cent of them trafficked are adolescent girls in the age group of 12 to 16 years. Dhar (2005) reports that 200,000 Bangladesh women trafficked during 1990-1997 and 5,000-7,000 Nepali women and girls illegally trafficked to India. This emphasis the need to combating trafficking on a war-footing and regulating migration, etc.

According to Patil (2006) there are 15 million children in bonded labour in India, 63 per cent of girls in Delhi have experienced child sexual abuse and there are 5,00,000 children in prostitution. This shows the enormity of child abuse and neglect, which need special attention. Further, he refers to the United Nations report on the First UN Secretary General's study of violence against children, which reveals that upto 80 to 98 per cent of children suffer from physical punishment in their homes, 150 million girls and 73 million boys under 18 years of age experience forced sexual intercourse or other forms of sexual violence during 2002. Further, from 2000 onwards. 1.8 million children were forced into prostitution and pornography and 1.2 million were victims of trafficking, child abuse, violence and neglect or all evils of society which have to be curbed immediately.

Anand (2006) says that "Foetal prejudice against the female child is manifested in the desire to have at least one male child to carry on the family name and lineage". In many cultures and countries, family preferences tend to favour boys over girls. 'Campaign against female foeticide' has been organized by different international, national and local agencies to sensitizing the community to accept the girl child, through educational programmes (Anand, 2006). The agencies have mainly focused on Gujarat, Rajasthan and U.P. The study of Anand reveals that 86.7 per cent desire 2 children wishing one boy and one girl. 68.9% of them feel that it is important to have a son as only he can perform the last rites. 93.3 per cent are aware of the fact that the sex of the child depends on the father and 91.1 per cent of the respondents are aware of the health problems arising from frequent abortions. It is also revealed that 97.8 per cent of the respondents are aware that sex determination in advance is illegal. The study highlights the need of repetitive interventions to change the mindset of people.

Government of India estimates that one in every 10 children is born with or acquires a physical, mental or sensory disability. More than 75% of disabilities are preventable. The situation of children with disabilities remains deplorable, particularly in rural areas and among the lower socio-economic strata. Also "Gender-discriminatory feeding and healthcare practices within the home render the girl child more vulnerable to ill health and acquired disabilities compared to her male counterparts (Renu, 2007) when poverty, physical neglect and social status intersect the impact on the disabled girl-child can be devastating. Disabled girls are kept hidden away at home and denied the basic rights of mobility, education and employment and viewed as dependent and a life-long burden on the natal family. The disabled persons need dignity of respect, inclusion, participation, equalization of opportunities and empowerment. Only 8% disabled children are enrolled in schools. The rest 98.2% are out of school, leading vague lives. A large number of persons with disability have no access to basic needs like health, education, livelihood, medical rehabilitation, recreation and other essential services (http://www.ishwar.ngo.org/facts.htm).

Ali (2008) mentions the facts in her article that "world wide, two million girls between ages 5-15 years are introduced into the commercial sex market each year. In India, one crime is committed against women every three minutes, one act of sexual harassment, eve-teasing every 53 minutes and one rape every 29 minutes, further 84 per cent of these persons known to the victim", which clearly shows that the crimes against women and girls have been increasing. So that, the role of different sections of the society like family members, self-help groups, panchayats, health workers, social workers, legal support becomes very important in dealing with the problem of violence against women.

Many girls and boys live in and around the Baruipur railway platform. Some are homeless while others have indifferent or abusive parents forcing them to seek shelter on the platform. As there is also a red light area nearby, these children are easily coerced into prostitution. According to Bahuguna (2006), Kolkata based NGO, Sanlaap, has started a unique intervention on the Baruipur railway platform with the aim of preventing child prostitution. The author observes that "these children on 'platform' face every kind of abuse including sex and used to sell drugs like ganja, etc., by the traders on the platform and local dons. So these children need special intervention and programmes to overcome from all sorts of abuses.

Equality of sexes is a fundamental right under the constitution of India. Gender equality means the belief in the equality of the sexes. Equality does not mean that all human beings are equal mentally and physically. It signifies equality of status and equality of opportunity. Gafoor (2008) conducted a study of gender equality beliefs among rural and urban boys and girls. The sample comprised 285 girls and 205 boys from rural areas and 135 girls and 78 boys from urban areas the study revealed that urban boys have the least commitment to gender equality. Rural girls have internalized this value better than their urban counterparts. Boy groups felt that males are better leaders. All the groups favour 'Women Reservation' and they are also against selective abortion. Further, the study identified that 58 per cent of adolescent believe that widow marriage is to be encouraged. However, 42 per cent are against it. The study concludes that even after successful completion of ten years of schooling, the younger generation retains the gender bias but education aspires to rootout such bias. The present system of education has to undergo scientifically planned modification to create a more gender egalitarian society.

The imposition of ban on sex determination clinics, 'has not deterred the doctors from holding the test. Similarly, female foeticide is rampant deposits warnings. A recent survey by Asian age (2008) has shown that the capital's high profile South Delhi area has an all-time low sex ratio of 762.

Manjula (2008) while discussing reasons for desertion of wife by husband mentions that "If the woman gives birth only to girls, she is disrespected and sometimes discarded and man marries again to be get a son".

GIRL CHILD PSYCHOLOGICAL DEVELOPMENT

Bielawska et al. (1996) compare in their study maternal and parental perceptions of 3 month-old infants. The data is collected from 172 couples aged 16-43 years with the help of 6 questionnaires. Some determinants of perception are different when father's and mother's views of their children's characters and behaviour are analyzed separately. Fathers of boys perceive their babies more positively than fathers of girls. Negative parental perception is related to the social support they receive.

Silverstein, et al., (1998) related 377, 17 to 25 years old female college students' reports of symptomatology to their reports of parental attitudes suggesting limitations inherent in being female. Subjects completed a scale measuring their perceptions that their fathers would have been prouder of them if they were male and scale measuring their distress over the limitations experienced by their mothers. So who scored high on either scale exhibited much higher prevalence than other subjects of self-reported depression accompanied by anxiety, somatic symptoms including headaches, insomnia, dyspepsea, fatigue, disordered eating and poor body image/preference for thinness. Further, the authors compared to 191 same aged (age-matched) and found that female, subjects exhibited much higher prevalence of anxious somatic depression.

Behavioural psychologists are finally convinced that the personality of an individual is governed by early childhood experiences. Bhogle (1999) in her study deals with development of two behaviours namely, aggression and dependency in girl children and relates them to discriminating child-rearing practices. Two hundred and ninety pre-school age (3-6 years) children drawn from 30 schools spread over a metropolitan city, semi-urban locations and village background with three economic groups. The children are observed for two behaviours and their parents are interviewed for child-rearing practices and parental attitudes towards the girl child. Further, the results reveal that there is significant discrimination in feeding, weaning and toilet-training practices, as well as parental attitudes towards the girl child. But the major discrimination is in the areas of sending the girl child to school, choice of school and her future aspirations. The girls are noted be dependent while the boys are aggressive and independent. The mothers love the children equally. But still, the author notices a difference in the parental attitudes. This is because they generally believe that girls should not be treated in the same way as boys, as they have to be trained for their difficult adult role as wife and mother. The traditional belief that boys need to be cared and nurtured more because they carry the family name, and care for parents during their old age, has a hold on them.

Psychology of adolescence covers various aspects of development like physical, intellectual, emotional, religious and moral aspects. If the student is well adjusted during the adolescence period he/she will become a good and adjusted adult. Yadav et al. (2005) studied the status of identity style among male and female college students and their adjustment in different environments. A sample of 225 male and female students drawn randomly from Bangur Nagar, a Senior College in Dharwad, Karnataka. The identity style inventory and the adjustment inventory in group were used to collect the data. The results of the study revealed that 96 per cent of the college students had developed identity style. Majority 93%, 79%, 76% and 73% of the college students were satisfied with their home, social, educational and emotional adjustment the information style was negatively related to home adjustment. Among female students, 36.89 per cent had average home adjustment whereas, 33.67 per cent boys had good home adjustment 37.33 per cent female students had unsatisfactory and 49.78 boys had average social adjustment. 44.44 per cent of female students and 51.11 per cent of boys had good educational adjustment. Regarding emotional adjustment, 42.6 per cent male students, 65.78 per cent female students had average adjustment. On the whole, more male students are satisfied with home, social and emotional adjustment than female students and more female students are satisfied with educational adjustment.

Children grow fast and acquire knowledge during childhood. The development of human personality rests on the sound foundation of social, emotional, physical and intellectual development of the child built during the stages of infancy and school-going age. Consequently failure or lacuna in any one of these steps affects the whole personality of the child (Sulthan and Velayuthan, 2006).

Mahajan and Sharma (2006) in their study examined the mental health status, school adjustment and scholastic achievement of adolescents in single parent families with reference to gender and family structure. The sample comprised 93 adolescents and their single mothers. Data was gathered using developmental psychopathology checklist of children, school adjustment inventory and the scholastic achievement record of the adolescents. Results were analysed using Multivariate ANOVA and Pearson's correlation. The results revealed that no differences existed in the mental health status and school adjustment of adolescents by gender. However, significant gender differences were evident for scholastic achievement. Regarding family structure, adolescents from nuclear families were significantly better adjusted in school than their counterparts from single parent families. The results also indicated that adolescents who had better mental health status were better adjusted and achieved more in schools. The study suggests planning of intervention strategies and undertaking active research on guidance and counselling involving mothers and adolescents in single parent's families.

The rising phenomenon of single parent families and their impact on family dynamics and the wellbeing of individual members is concern of research. Mahajan and Sharma (2006) say that countries like United States of America (24 per cent) the former Soviet Union (21 per cent) and Sweden (17 per cent) have reported the highest rate of single parent families. The authors conducted a study with a sample of 93 adolescents and their single mothers. Data was gathered using Developmental Psychopathology Check List of Children, School Adjustment Inventory and Scholastic Achievement record of the adolescents. The results revealed that no differences existed in the mental health status and school adjustment of adolescent by gender. However, significant gender differences were evident for scholastic achievement. Regarding scholastic achievement girls perform better than boys. The study suggests to undertake active research on guidance and counselling to involving mothers and adolescents of single parent families.

Sharma Subhangana (2007d) in her study "Empowerment of Rural girl child for quality life" anlaysed rural girl child status and identified the areas of empowerment to develop interventions. The study identified that the girl child is over-burdened with household work and farm activities with little support from the family, discriminated in areas of food, clothing and have no knowledge of their rights. 112 girls were selected from five villages from Bhawarna block. After selection of the sample, the girls were pretested for socio-economic status, self-esteem, 16 personal factors, learning styles, Raven progressive matrices, communication skills, legal status and general awareness. Further, intervention in areas legal, general, etc., through stories, discussion and lectures for two and half months. The results revealed that the girls performed better after intervention. Further, it was identified from the results that the girls acquired knowledge of legal privileges available for girls and also recognized the need to develop self-esteem and self-reliance.

Adolescence is a stage of development in various areas and corresponding adjustments and adolescents need maximum attention and care of their parents. Saini (2007) undertook to investigate the psychological problems of adolescent children of Chandigarh. In urban areas, adolescent children face personal and social problems due to changing life-style of the city and competition in the field of education and vocation. A sample of 415 adolescents was drawn randomly from 8 government and private schools of Chandigarh, the results identified that adolescent children faced maximum problems in the areas of Social Recreational Activities (SRA), personal Psychological Relations (PPR), Social Psychological Relations (SPR) and Adjustment to College Work (ACW). All the respondents in the study had psychological problems, but their experiences of problems in different areas were of varying intensity. The findings of the present study highlight the need of counselling and support services to adolescents in facilitating their development by teachers and parents.

Adolescence is a state of storm and stress. The need of counselling services for students at school, college and universities should not be minimized or denied. According to Das (2007) adolescent boys and girls experience emotional disturbances. In order to reduce anxiety and tension they may go for psychoactive drugs like cocaine, heroin, etc., which are injected into the blood vessel with a common syringe for quick comfort. Human Immunodeficiency Virus (HIV) may be thus transmitted from infected persons to non-infected persons through the common syringe. Thus, both the dangerous evils i.e., drug addiction and Acquired Immune Deficiency Syndrome spread like wild fire allover. They can be prevented by imparting proper counselling to them at schools, colleges and universities.

The role-modelling aspect of television and movies although frequently overlooked, is crucial to understanding its influence on children, in particular. They learn to behave by imitating attractive role models. Mathur and Verma (2007) conducted a study to assess the attitude of adolescents towards violence and aggression shown in movies. They cited "more than 1000 scientific studies and reviews" to conclude that significant exposure to media violence increases the risk of aggressive behaviour in children and adolescents". A questionnaire was administered to 100 adolescents (50 male and 50 female) of 16-18 years to collect the data. The study revealed that a majority of the adolescents feel that movies are disseminating much more than a fair amount of violence and aggression, directly and indirectly influencing the youth. Further, the results shows that 66 per cent of adolescents feel that movies are motivating and suggesting new methods of crime to the youth, far 60 per cent movies show too much of violence and aggression, 88% adolescent feel that the terrorism shown in movies is unjustifiable and 34 per cent are eager to adopt the behaviour shown in the movies.

Dubey et al. (2008) carried out a study on the impact of Information and Communication Technology (ICT) on school students" in a leading school in Bangalore. The school has been a front runner in terms of use of technology and its accessibility. The school is chosen so as to get a better understanding of the impact of ICT since other schools lack the required infrastructure and technical manpower. The study reveals that there is a positive impact of ICT on seven identified components. It shows that all components of the education system like students, parents, administrators, perceive ICD as a useful and friendly tool which have a positive impact on students and the education system. An average of over 79 per cent of the students, 80 per cent of parents, 71 per cent of teachers perceive that the use of ICT has improved the learning of students. 74 per cent students, 69 per cent parents, 69 per cent of teachers feel that the use of ICT has improved the behaviour of the students who have become more responsible and disciplined etc.

Adolescence is a transitional period of one's life between childhood and adulthood, during which some important biological, psychological and social changes take place. It is a period of storm and stress. Adolescents have to adjust with their own changes in personality on one side and changing socio-economic environment on the other side. Some adolescents find it difficult to adjust normally with these changes and experience some problems, which are characteristic of this developing stage. Talukdar and Talukdar

(2008) conducted a study of 200 adolescent students 100 male and 100 female of class Xi and XII, age 16 to 19 years to assess their level of adjustment in areas, home, health, social, emotional and educational, and to identify the major factors responsible for it. The study reveals that the overall adjustment of male students was found to be better than that of female students. Social adjustment was average in both groups. The results also shows unsatisfactory adjustment of female adolescents in different areas under the study. Emotional adjustment of both male and female groups is found to be unsatisfactory. Home and health adjustment of female students is found to be unsatisfactory. The author feel that overprotection, over permissiveness, too much of strictness, lack of money are some factors responsible for students adjustmental problems at home. This study reveals that adolescent students sought counselling to solve their personal problems, emotional, educational, home, health and social adjustment.

Adolescence is a transitional phase that faces a wide range of developmental issues. Character building or personality development in a person depends mainly on how the developmental need of each stage of life, especially adolescence, is met. In today's fast moving world, all individuals are stressed with their own personal and professional demands. Naachimuthu and Rekha (2008) attempt to identify the various guidance needs of adolescent children. A total of 935 school-going adolescents aged 13 to 17 years from various schools between 7th to 10th class in Hyderabad city were selected as sample. The Guidance Need Inventory (GNI) developed by Grewal, 1982 was administered to them which assessed the guidance need of the students on five dimensions viz., physical, psychological, social, educational and vocational. The results showed that the guidance needs of the students of adolescent boys and girls differ. Boys have more psychological guidance needs while girls have more educational guidance needs. The physical needs (86.7%) and psychological needs (75.9%) are greater in the school-going adolescents whose parents (both) are employed than in the case of those with a single parent.

Children with conduct problems have deficiencies in social skills, anger control, interpersonal problem solving and moral reasoning and remediation of these skills will lead to improved functioning and better outcomes. Anuradha (2008) conducted a study to promote social competency in a group of children with conduct problems, and to study self-perception of children before and after the group work intervention. The results reveal that the total mean scores of self-perception have increased from 41.66 to 66.33 after the intervention. Thus, on the whole it can be observed that there has been a significant change in the perception of 'self' of the boys (rural) after participating in the group work.

Girl Child Exploitation

The literacy rate varies from urban to rural and men to women. According to Sen and Drenze (1995) the girl child suffers the most because of the willful and criminal neglect of basic education of the elitist tendencies of the ruling cultural and religious traditions in India, may have added to the problem. The status of the girl child constitutes a problem in almost all the states of India and has emerged today as a fundamental question of human resource development. In India, domestic burden on the girl child is always higher than on male child both in rural and urban areas. A survey conducted by the C.I.N.T. showed that 55 per cent girls do household work against only 15 per cent of boys. The paid and unpaid work keeps the girls away from school and they have practically no leisure to enjoy their childhood.

Son preference is the biggest hurdle in the way of girl child's right to exist. But, according to Raj Bhanti (1995) some tribals who too prefer soon have their own reasons for it. However, girls in tribal communities are neither discriminated against nor unwanted. The girl child does not suffer deprivation in the vital spheres of nutrition and health. The data collected by the author indicates that tribal girls may be relatively disadvantaged in the educational sphere and they are forced into work to earn livelihood. In addition to the household work load the girls have to toil. The study reveals that girls of 6-11 years of age were not enrolled in schools. Enrollment in the ages of 11-14 was 29 per cent for girls as against 54 per cent for boys. Obviously the girl child in this community has to work more and in hazardous occupations also. But this is not because of sex discrimination but because of escalating costs of the basic necessities of life and lack of minor forest products. Among tribals, girls are not entitled to inherit property. If parents do not have son, property will go to a close relative but not to a daughter.

Girls are confined to home to do household work and are trained for future married life and child-rearing. Boys and girls are treated differently in family and society. The socialization of girls is heavily influenced by the institution of family, marriage and kinship. Deprivation of basic education is one of the worst forms of human rights violation. There are gaps between enrollment rates of boys and girls in developing countries (Pal, 1997). Further, India has the largest illiterate population in the world. Vulnerable groups are often deprived of educational opportunities.

According to UNICEF (1997) 140 million children (23 per cent) in the developing countries in the age group of 6 to 11 years do not go to school. According to official statistics, 13 million children are faced to do dangerous or exploitative work to support their families. Unofficial estimates put the number of children affected by child labour at 100 million (www.savethechildren.in/india). Save the children organization in co-operation with parents and teachers, have increased the number of children enrolling in schools across or project areas by reaching over to 800 children in Jammu and Kashmir in 2006 alone. Though child labour is a global problem it has become a serious problem in the developing countries like India. In our country, 40 per cent of the population are children, out of this 25 per cent are engaged in child labour. Poverty, illiteracy, unemployment, social customs, population explosion and low income of parents are the chief causes which have forced children to work as labourers.

Every social grouping in the world has specific traditional and cultural practices and beliefs. Some customs are beneficial to all the members, while others are harmful to a specific group, such as women and children. The traditional cultural practices reflect the values and beliefs held by members of a community. Balingar (1999) says that "In recent times, the low status of the girl child in India has received much attention. Press reports and studies have pointed to the prevalence of discrimination against the girl child not only by men but even by women including mothers". There is thus an urgent need to change the negative attitudes of the family, especially those of mothers, in order to ameliorate the condition of the girl child.

Misra (1999) in his study found that 63 per cent of child-workers belong to the general castes and 37 per cent belong to the SC and ST. Nearly 60 per cent of girl workers are in the age group of 10-14 years and are mostly engaged at the time of sowing and harvesting of paddy, etc.. They generally work for nine to ten hours for Rs. 15 to 20 per day. Further, the girl child in the age group of 5-10 years is engaged for cleaning cattle shed, cattle grazing, collection of cow dung, etc., and are paid Rs. 60 to 90 per month, and they are mostly SC and ST girl child workers. Further, 67 per cent of girl workers are physically and mentally tortured by male workers and servants engaged by the land-owners.

Girls begin to participate in domestic work earlier than boys. They may also be made to do heavier chores than boys such as fetching and carrying water, gathering fuel, heading cattle and buffaloes. But they may not be given chance or opportunity as their brothers as potential wage-earners.

Young girls are engaged in various small-scale industries and cottage industries and they contribute their mite to the needs of the family. Yet they are regarded as an economic burden, because their savings do not meet the requirement of dowry and the expenditure on their marriage and traditional post-marriage gifts (Nayar, 1999). A major point of contrast between girls and boys engaged early in domestic non-economic work is that while boys eventually move on to full-time agricultural or wage earning labour, young girls continue to shoulder the burden of household tasks, from where they are relegated eventually to their roles as wives and mothers.

According to Santha (2000) and the M.V. Foundation a study was carried out report on "Impact of Girl Child's enrollment on work-sharing and distribution pattern in families "to know the socio-economic conditions of the families of the erstwhile girl child labourers and to know about the change and adjustments, if any, taking place in the family. The study was conducted in 109 villages in 14 mandals and 225 households of the erstwhile girl child labourers were inducted into the education process through the M.V. Foundation Camps. At the time of survey, out of the sample 67 girls were studying in M.V.F. Camps, 127 girls were in government hostels or residential schools and 31 girls were continuing their studies at the local school. The study noticed that there was a wholesome change in the attitude of parents and other family members towards the girls and their education. Parents were showing more affection to girls. Many parents in the study area now give much importance to child's education and wish to see their daughters as good employees in future.

Bangladesh is an agro-based country in South Asia with limited natural resources and vast human power. Most of the people of this country are living below the poverty level. About 74.4 million female population live in this country, 37 per cent of them aged less than 15 years. The advancement of girls and women has been on the agenda of many governments in the last decades (Ministry of Planning, Bangladesh, 2003).

Deb (2005) studied a group of 120 migrant child labours working in households, tea stalls, garages and shops in south Kolkata and found that an overwhelming number of children were abused, in some way or the other physically, mentally and sexually. The 120 children studied (75 boys and 45 girls) were in the age group between 10 to 16 years who had migrated from rural areas were and working as maidservants, in shops, tea stalls and garages. The study found that 45.8 per cent of them were illiterate, 53.3 per cent were involved in domestic work and 53.3 per cent were paid Rs. 201-400/- per month. Further the study revealed that 42.55 per cent were victims of mental torture, 35.5 per cent physical torture and 10.8 per cent harassed sexually. Both physical abuse and sexual harassment were more prevalent among girl children. Child abuse in different forms and neglect is thus a frequent occurrence on working children.

In India, child labour is a violation of our constitutional commitment to social and, economic justice, equality of opportunity and dignity of the individual. Yet, many children are engaged in various occupations and processing units etc., Goyal (2005) found in his study that the Ludiana hosiery industry, extensively used child labour which contributed about 30 per cent of the total industrial production of the state. Goyal studied 137 child labours working in the hosiery industry. His study revealed that 50 per cent of the respondents belonged to families living below the poverty line. In 20.44 per cent of the cases the child was the sole wage-earner in the family. Most of the respondents stated that they were working in a very poor working environment, which affected them physically and psychologically, 31.11 per cent of the child workers reported that they were ill-treated by their employer. Further, the children were also exploited by their parents to make short and narrow gains. The parents usually secured loans from employers and surrendered their children as security. The results of the study suggested there is a need of strict enforcement of child labour laws for the well-being of the children.

Mondal et. al. (2006) investigated the progressive movements of women in different sectors of Bangladesh. The results signified that there was an increase in the school attendance rate of girls in female participation in the workforce, and the fertility rate had declined dramatically along with improved maternal mortality.

Child labour is mainly a socio-economic problem, several factors are responsible for it. According Yadav (2006) apart from poverty the other associated factors like unequal distribution of land and other resources, illiteracy, unemployment, social structure, demand of cheap and docile children in the market etc., are responsible for the growth of child labour. All these factors are interwoven in a vicious circle. The author says that children's participation in labour activities is largely confined to unorganized sectors where they are left unnoticed. About 77 per cent child workers are engaged in agriculture and cultivation, which is literally out of the purview of the labour laws and very young and tender children are made to work. The study also examined child-workers conditions in three different sectors in different states i.e., agriculture in Ananthapur, match and fire works in Sivakashi, and glass and bangle factors in Firozabad. It was found that families forced their children to work due to poverty and lack of agricultural land. They had migrated and were struggling to survive in the new environment. These families utilized their human resources namely their children by involving them in work. Nearly 65 per cent of the families get one thousand rupees a month through their children. Further the study found that children worked for nearly seven to ten hours a day, without proper rest. To address this social evil (child labour) comprehensive and joint efforts Government and Non-Government Organisations are required. Besides rehabilitative approach, prohibitive and preventive approach need to be seriously implemented.

The future of any nation depends upon the sound development of its children. According Shukla and Ali (2006) for building a civilized, cultured and happy society, we have to educate and train our children properly because tomorrow they would take the nation towards prosperity. The elimination of child labour, their rehabilitation has emerged as an important area of scientific work. It has been seen that a large number of child labourers are surviving under great health and safety hazards. Further, work place trauma is widespread, stunting the growth of the child both physically and mentally. Hence considering the problem in its totality, an effort has to made to protect the rights of children and provide essential interventions.

The educational system in India is highly stratified across gender, caste, class, region and religion. However, gender remains the most pervasive axis of educational stratification and disparities in India. Alam's study (2007) tries to capture gender disparity in a multi-dimensional and analytical frame work. The study brings out some interesting findings, such as: when the education of the head of the household/parents crossed a certain threshold level, girl's education receives several impetuses. Similarly, girls of those in white collar jobs stand equal chances of schooling compared to boys. As compared to the children of cultivators, those of agricultural labourers have 3.135 times lesser chances to be enrolled in schools. Households having a lower level of education as is the case with farming and non-farming self-employed houses, are also found to be espousing traditional social values, where sending daughters after puberty outside the house is considered neither socially good nor desirable. This results in the withdrawal of girls from school after the elementary level.

According Ranjan (2009) displacements due to communal riots, terrorism, naxalites, Maoists, ethnic conflicts, natural calamities, etc., affect the life of the people as well as their children. When displacement takes place, the family members may get scattered over various places. "The large-scale displacement of families during the Naga-Kuki ethnic conflicts in 1995-96 witnessed disorientation of social and economical life in the affected regions of Manipur. The conflict also saw massive human migration to the Imphal Valley, many of whom were children who had been rendered homeless and orphaned. As there were no adequate rehabilitation efforts from the government, many of these helpless children became unskilled labourers for their livelihood. With figures from varied scores giving the verdict, India is known to have the largest number of working children in the world. A research study carried out by "Save the Children" (2005), shows that 74 per cent of child domestic workers in India are in the age group of 12 to 16 years, most of them are working for measly wages.

GIRL CHILD RIGHTS

Development of the girl child is the first phase of enhancement of women's status "Today's girl child is tomorrow's woman". If tomorrow's woman are to become equal partners with men in bringing about social change and development, this is the time to accord the girl child her rightful share of human dignity and opportunity (World Declaration on Survival, Protection and Development of Children 1990). Equal opportunities should be provided for the girl child to benefit from the health, nutrition, education and other basic services to enable her to grow to her full potential.

Gokhale (1995) in his article "Girl child, her rights and law" discusses the legal rights of the girl child. The girl of today is the woman of tomorrow when she becomes an able and effective partner with man social development can be achieved. Further, the author stresses the need to provide legal support as well as protect her basic rights of education, security etc., to the girl child.

Eminent social activists draw our attention to the subtle aspects of our concern for the girl child and suggest measures to support the girl child. Sharma (1995) discusses the discrimination practiced against the girl child in SAARC region and suggests strategies for intervention. He says that, rights may be declared and policies formulated to express our collective liberal and human's concern, but unless the real life of the girl child in her family and community is touched by tangible efforts and actions nothing can be achieved. Further, effective implementation of laws to protect the girl child rights is to be ensured.

According to Vandana (1998), "Since India's ratification of the convention on the Right of the Child, some ground has been gained in terms of awareness and action towards the same. Still 53 per cent of our under-five-year children are malnourished, 60 million children under six years still live below the poverty line, 45 million are known to be wage-earners and 2 million children die every year before reaching two years of age".

Andal (1999) says: every woman in India is caught in a vicious circle. As a child she is make to fed that she is unwanted and a liability. When she becomes a mother and begets a daughter, she herself perpetuates the injustices she has suffered and teaches her girl child to be a subservient and self-sacrificing person, who undervalues herself. This process repeats itself time and again. We need to break this cycle. Girl child, the mother of tomorrow, needs to be vigilant and support must be given to change the face of Indian society.

Lack of education, mounting consumerism combined with the demand for dowry, poverty, inadequate knowledge of family planning and insufficient of facilities for family planning, and the greed of doctors have all compounded to create the crises of infanticide and foeticide. According Ninapuri (1999), only a minority of girls in India, who are visibly are enjoying equal opportunities and equal love and care with boys. In order to facilitate this minority to become a majority, the Indian Government has enacted many laws in favour of the girl child.

Less participation in education limits the personal, social and intellectual horizons of girls. In India, half a billion women and girls are waiting for equality with men and improvement of their lives in life to lead life with dignity. The Mitakshara school of succession which was prevalent in most of North India, believed in the exclusive domain of male heirs. Priyadarshini and Tiwari (2000) point out that a number of State Amendments, have been made in the act effecting changes in the law relating to Mitakshra coparcenary declaring the daughter to be a coparcener in a joint Hindu family. The Constitution of India has proclaimed equality before law as a fundamental right.

Sharma (2004) has made an attempt to analyse the change of age at marriage, and to examine the level of knowledge of couples about the legal age at marriage. 500 couples were interviewed from four districts of Rajasthan. The results revealed that 59 per cent o the respondents had knowledge of it, but in rural areas, only 39 per cent were aware of it. Further, the study revealed that conventional beliefs regarding the virginity of a girl, economic factors, religious outlook, poor family condition and low education of parents were some of the reasons for early marriages in Rajasthan. Regarding child marriages the law would address only a part of the problem. The solution lies with the society itself. The Government and NGOs have to work together to stop child marriages by creating awareness and providing guidance to curb this practice of child marriages.

Efforts are needed to mobilize political, religious, cultural, administrative and community support for balancing the child sex ratio by changing the mindset of the people in favour of the girl child. Asha Bajpai (2007) says that, it was only during the 20th century that the concept of children's rights emerged. This shift in focus from the 'welfare' to the 'rights' approach is significant. Rights are entitlements. The rights approach is primarily concerned with issues of social justice, non-discrimination, equity and empowerment. The rights perspective is embodied in the United Nations Convention on the Rights of the Child (CRC), 1989, which is a land mark in international human right legislation. India ratified the convention on the rights of the child in December, 1992.

Violence against women and girls has been identified as gross violation of human rights, at national and international levels. Sarada and Lakshmi (2008) have discussed the contributing factors of violence. Political, economic, sociological, psychological factors, legal and other factors like alcoholism, indidelity of men, women's backwardness in education and income are some of the factors identified. Despite laws addressing violence against women at international level, national and judicial response, crimes against women are increasing year after year. A total of 1,64,765 incidents of crimes against women were reported in the country during 2006 which clearly indicates the in-effective law enforcement to deal with the cases of violence against women.

Girl Child Parental Support

Quraishi (1991) conducted a study of "Factor analysis of teachers' attitudes towards various groups and practices" using a sample of 200 secondary school teachers. The teachers included 120 men and 80 women with an average age of 38-48 years and 14-16 years of teaching experience. The study revealed that the teachers attitudes towards various groups and practices differed and the influencing factors were gender, social background etc.

Deb and Senapati (1993) identified four major modes of man-handling by the parents, such as physical torture, willful negligence, exploitation of innocence and dependency of the child. Further the study revealed five major aggravating factors for parents' cruelty and a socio-pathic family environment, viz., illiteracy, unemployment, conjugal discord, lack or attachment and history of victimization in the early life of parents Segal and Ashtekar (1994) found that 60 per cent of children ran away from home to avoid physical abuse.

Children are victimized with uncompromising parents wanting their children to skip schooling and instead adopt deceitful means of earning (Deb, 1994). Individuals cope with stresses in different ways. Some adopt strategies such as problem solving etc, whereas others respond by exhibiting negative attitude to things that is Burnout and Anger etc.

Wordsworth (1996) examines aspects of intergenerational facility relationships with the previous and the following generation which are likely to be affected by longer-term social and historical circumstances. The study examines 6 aspects of mid-life that may have been affected by childhood experience of social and family pressure for and against educational attainment, occupational attainment and satisfaction, satisfaction with family life, care of elderly parents, recall of own childhood etc. And the results reveal that there is a positive association between offspring's education and affection between mother and offspring and upbringing of the child.

Swarr et al., (1996) examined how young adolescent girls' pubertal development and perceptions of puberatal timing as well as their subjective experiences with their parents relate to the emergence of eating problems during later adolescence. The sample consisted of 240 white girls from 2 suburban communities near mid-western city. The results indicated that adolescent girl's positive relationships with both parents related to heath per eating scores, both concurrently and longitudinally.

The relationship between the gender of children in a family and their parent's gender-role attitudes in Japan is examined by Kamo and Worner (1997) and the findings indicate that parents with daughter have less egalitarian gender-role attitudes. Japanese parents would try to reduce cognitive dissonance of their daughters' structural positions by accepting gender inequalities. Victimization of children take place mostly in economically disadvantaged families.

The gender-role attitudes of girls, includes their ideas of mother hood as well as their ideas of female roles in general. Carine and Janssens (1998) examined the relations between mother's employment status and their level of education and daughters, gender role attitudes mediated by mother's own gender role attitudes and child-rearing style. 165 adolescent girls aged 15-22 years and their mothers mean age 45-99 years participated in the study. On the whole, the data demonstrates the importance of mothers in the development of daughter's gender-role attitudes. A mother's child-rearing style as well as her own gender-role attitudes do influence the gender-role attitudes a daughter develops. Mother's level of education and employment have indirect effects.

Barbara and Theressa (1999) examined mother's and father's communications to sons and daughters in 48 families during both a free play episode and their teaching the child playground behaviour, that posed some threat to safety because of the child's developmental status. The results revealed that mothers and fathers responded similarly to each other, but differently to sons and daughters, the coding of physical contact revealed that parents applied more pressure on sons than daughters to attempt the pole task without physical assistance and provided more spontaneous physical assistance to daughters than sons. The results suggested that parents communicate with young children in different ways that may promote greater risk-taking by boy and greater perceived to reduce injury vulnerability among girls. This clearly show that parents train and encourage boys rather than girls to take-up difficult and risky tasks.

Joshi (2005) says that "study of the emotional reactions and emotional anxieties in relation to examinations, abilities, interactions, affiliations and actualization is important for guiding students who are from different families". He studied 200 students (selecting 100 students each from high income and low income groups and from each stratum 50 boys and 50 girls) the data was collected with the help of self-developed tool 'Manifest anxiety scale'. The data revealed that students from the higher economic stratum were more in the categories of 'anxious about higher performance' (76.77%), 'inconsistencies in the loyalty' (73.83%), 'non-acceptance by the peer group' (62.83%) and 'failure of family support' (57.80%). Further the study revealed that students from the low economic stratum were more in categories of 'anxious about non-observance of morals', (77.70%), 'not coping with expectations of the teacher' (75.33%) and 'failure of family support' (74.60%). The study results stress the need of proper understanding of students' anxieties and need of teachers and parents guidance for better adjustment in society.

Mental illness of a parent may also put stress on the relationships in a family and this may adversely affect the child. According to Philip and Parashar (2006) the researches done in the past have indicated that children who have a parent with mental illness are at a significantly greater risk for multiple psychological problems. The authors conducted a study of 36 children (18 boys and 18 girls) in the age group of 10 to 19 years. It revealed statistically significant difference in family satisfaction and subjective wellbeing between boy and girl. However, family satisfaction and subjective wellbeing of adolescent children did not differ depending on the sex of the affected parent. In the study 96.9 per cent of the adolescent children were found to be dissatisfied with their family environment. The study highlights the need of intervention programmes to address mental health needs and life skills development programmes for these vulnerable children. An adolescent who is no longer a child and is not yet an adult is an important area in the study of human behaviour.

The basic needs of a child are love, security, independence and adventure. Very few blind children are able to have them. Some parents do every thing for the blind child and burden themselves with more work without even allowing the blind child to stretch their wings and be independent. This leads the blind child, into more frustration. Singhe and Kazi (2006) study was aimed at knowing the perceived parental attitudes towards blind children. A sample of 40 blind children from the 6-18 years age group were selected from centres of Gulbarga. Pre-designed interview schedule and participation observation were employed to collect the required information. It was found from the study that 55 per cent of the sample were discriminated against and ill-treated by their parents, in comparison to their sighted children. The children reported that their parents felt it burden to have such disabled children. The plight of the blind girl child is worse. They were more discriminated against then their boy counterparts. Further, it is revealed that a majority (60 per cent) of the parents felt apathy, guilt and shame for having a blind child. Their attitude to these handicapped children has ambiguous. It is unfortunate that such as attitude was found even more among the educated and well-off parents.

In a receptive child learning takes place all the time. However at the stage of childhood it is very concentrated. An impediment to any aspect of this learning creates problems for the young child. Parikh (2006) made an attempt to study the effect of self-esteem on peer relations, with a sample of 34 students from a south Mumbai school. The results revealed that positive marked correlation was seen in both groups of children i.e., children with learning disability (16), and children without learning disability (18) indicating that peer relationship improves healthier self-esteem and deteriorates with lower self esteem. Regarding self-esteem and peer relations, there is no difference between children with learning disability and those without. The author summarises that this is probably a direct result of the active support of parents and the school.

Children grow faster and acquire more knowledge during childhood. The development of human personality rests on sound foundation of social, emotional, physical and intellectual development of the child laid during the stages of infancy and school-going age. Consequently failure or lacuna in any one of these steps affects the whole personality of the child (Sulthan and Velayutham, 2006).

Goswami (2006) conducted a study of the expectations of children from their teachers, parents, community etc., the data was collected from the states of North East India (7 states). The analysis revealed that a majority of children expected love and affection from parents (276), 169 understanding and encouragement and 127 guidance. Regarding expectations from teachers. 73 expected guidance, love and affection by 36, understanding and encouragement by 29, and values to be taught to them by 36. Regarding expectation from society as many as 122 wanted society to stay united, co-operation by 113, maintenance of peace and security by 999 which corresponds to good governance. The results reflect the understanding of the role of the teachers by the children, as they expect to be taught values and given guidance etc., they also show the need of teacher to teach about life and guide to achieve these goals.

Occupational stresses like, workload, role ambiguity and conflict, inadequate resources. Staff conflicts etc have been associated with higher levels of Burnout, distress. Aley's (2008) study is an attempt to understand how burnout and anger in teachers and parents affect the development of children. 45 teachers, who are also parents, from two different schools were selected for the study and administered Maslach Burnout Inventory - Human services survey, Self Monitoring Form for Anger and Life Experiences Questionnaire on them. The results revealed that 20 per cent of the sample fall under the high range category on Emotional Exhaustion and 40 per cent high on diminished personal accomplishment and 10 per cent high on Depersonalization. Headache is recorded as the main physical symptom during or after anger experiences. Further, many teachers admitted beating their children in order to make them obey or to teach them discipline. The author stresses that teacher-parents have a double emotional burden to carry. To overcame the problem, schools and colleges need to have an atmosphere of team-work among the staff and other supportive services like counselling, personality development etc.

This research work clearly indicates need to create an awareness among parents to provide a healthy environment for their blind children. It emphasizes the need of counselling the blind to mould their personality in an integral way. Hearing impairment or deafness is one of the most severe of all disabilities because it strikes at a basic human function i.e., communication. Limaye (2008) in her article examines how young girls with hearing impairment respond to the developmental tasks of adolescence. Using the study approach she explores the attitudes of adolescent girls and finds that adolescent girls with hearing impairment face the same developmental needs and tasks that confront hearing impaired adolescents. Instead of submitting meekly to their disability and the authority of their families, both clients emerge as self-assertive, individualised and spirited persons who contest popular negative stereo types of persons with disabilities. This study supports that girls with hearing impairment based on family support to develop self-confidence and assertiveness.

In a countrywide study, Centre for Women's Development studies in India (2008), sought information of the girl child's socialization process in the family. The sample comprised 13,000 girls and their mothers, drawn from rural and urban areas. The data revealed that 57 per cent mothers were non-literate, only 2 per cent of the parents expected or desired a girl, 77.5 per cent of girls shared household work with the mother as compared only 0.5 per cent of boys who shared work with the father. 75 per cent of girls had never been out of their village on work, pilgrimage or picnics, 77 per cent of the girls felt that literacy is important for both boys and girls, and 60 per cent of girls felt that they had no skills. They believed that all the tasks that they carried out did not need any skill.

Girl Child Welfare

In a developing society, education and health are the parameters to analyse the level of development to the society has achieved. According to Rekha (1995), every tribal child is prone to disease, since conception, because the immunization of pregnant tribal women is at a very low level in tribal society. Though there are strong evidences of good work done by NGOs, social workers and government hospitals, the overall picture however is far from satisfactory. Crude methods of deliveries, low immunization, lack of proper medical attention and low nutritious feedings, absence of adequate mother care make the child more susceptible to diseases. Owing to inadequate food intake and hard work the girl child gets diseases very easily. Tuberculosis, loss of eye-sight and other water borne diseases are quite common among the tribal girls.

The world's largest school lunch programme, "mid-day-meal" was launched on 15th August, 1995 in India on a limited scale. The programme covered 8.5 lakh primary and upper primary schools of the entire country. The basic idea was to increase enrollment, ensure attendance and retention of children of the age group of 6-14 years, simultaneously improve the nutritional status of children at the primary and upper primary stage in Government and local bodies and aided schools. The scheme is yielding excellent results. Not only the enrollment has increased but also the dropout rate has decreased. It has also created a congenial atmosphere in schools which is necessary for learning because only a healthy child will learn better and faster.

Khan's study (2004) of 1221 primary schools in 188 randomly selected villages in Bihar, Rajasthan, Madhya Pradesh, Uttar Pradesh reveals inadequate school facilities, lack of qualified women teachers, transport facilities, and hostel facilities for girls, fear of sexual harassment and fixed schooling hours are the serving as barrier to girls education. Further, the study reveals that 84 per cent schools do not have a toilet, and 54 per cent schools do not have drinking water facility. The results point up the urgency to take necessary steps to government to improve girl child's education.

Adolescent girl's in families are treated neither as children nor as young adults. And they hesitate to discuss certain issues with their parents. Majumdar (2006) describes a festival for girls known as Kishori Utsav. Over 1500 adolescent girls from 10 districts and Uttar Pradesh participated in it. The programme was organized by Mahila Samakhya to address the problems of adolescent rural girls. During this programme, the girls shed many of their inhibitions and nervousness to discuss their hopes dreams and fears. The programme helped the girls to ask questions they had never been able to ask at home and also provided an opportunity to understand them better.

Vidyasagar (2007) discusses the situation of education particularly of girls, in his paper "Educational inequality and teacher performance in Andhra Pradesh: Challenges ahead". He examines all the developments that impinge upon the prevailing educational scenario in the state. He points out that the literacy rate increased from 44.1 per cent in 1991 to about 73 per cent by 2001. There was increasing budget allocation for construction of 45,000 buildings, establishing 26.723 schools, recruitment of 1.76 lack school teachers, improving sanitary conditions in about 55,000 schools and distributing about 3 lack bicycles to school-going girls as part of the 'Soukaryam' scheme. Programe 'Chaduvulapanduga', 'Malle Badiki' and 'Akshara Jyothi', etc., had led to huge enrollment of children in schools. Further, the state has undertaken a girl child protection scheme to provide specific initiatives to encourage education for girls. The author thinks that if the girl child protection scheme is extended to a large number of girls children on condition that she does not marry until the legal age of 18 years, the initiatives taken would be successful.

3

Methodology

Indian is a signatory and member of International Instruments such as the UN convention on the rights of the child, with its two optional protocols, and convention on the elimination of all forms of discrimination against women (CEDAW) and girls, thereby affirming its commitment to the growth and development of women and children. However, "inadequate impact of programming investment and achievement in overall development of the girl child, and the adverse influence of negative social attitudes towards women and girls have left girl children in India disadvantaged" (Girl child in the Eleventh Five-year Plan 2007-2012). Their survival, development, well-being and participation as members of society in its development are a serious national concern.

Women's status is determined on female to male sex ratios of younger age groups in the population. The 2001 census of India highlighted a serious and worsening decline in the sex ratio in the 0-6 years age group, which was reflecting by unwillingness to give birth to a girl child, which leads to increase female foeticide and infanticide. Further it causes child marriages, girl child labour, prostitution, violences on girl child and deliberate neglect of girl children's health, nutrition, education and safety. "Research studies display that around 25% girls die in India before 15 years of age" (Tripati, 2005).

In India, a son is considered an investment, which will pay off the form of service and support to his parents in old age. A daughter on the other hand adds to the social burden of parents who would have to pay a heavy dowry a usual practice in most Indian households. Further, her contribution to the household economy is unacknowledged. The adverse attitude towards the girl child signals the catastrophe of serious demographic imbalance and degeneration of socio-economic conditions. Unfortunately, these days the rejection of girls begins even before their birth by prenatal sex determination tests which followed by quick abortions to eliminate female foetuses. In this male dominated society, girls are denied equal access to food, health care, education employment and human dignity along with boys.

The welfare of children, especially the girl child, depends on the opinion or attitudes of the parents, which are influenced by many socio-economic factors. "Opinion or attitude towards the girl child can be defined as the degree of positive or negative affect associated with the psychology of parents. Besides this, the parents' education, their socio-economic backgrounds, the nature of their employment and gender of the parents also influence their opinion about their girl child. There have been several studies of the girl child's status and problems (Leelamma Devasia and Devasia, 1991, Jasodhara et al., 2000, Mitabhadra, 1999, Mishra, 2000, Sisodia, 2003, Tripathy and Pradhan 2003). They cover many dimension of the problems of the girl child, i.e., girl child's education, girl child's status in low socio economic families etc. But, studies regarding the opinion of educated parents who are also teachers towards their girl child are scarce. Teachers play a crucial role in community motivation to enhance girls' access to education, and help in empowering girls. The predicament of the girl child especially in India is so deplorable and is of such magnitude that it seems almost impossible to remedy it, and give the girl child a better deal in life unless concerted efforts are constantly and continuously made by all concerned to ameliorate the situation of girl children. One of the most important and urgent things to be done is to work towards achieving attitudinal change towards them and eradicate permanently prejudices against them and false notions about them. In this stupendous task teachers can and have to play a leading role, because they can make a lasting impact on the growing and impressionable minds of their pupils at school who look to them for guidance and regard them as role models. Hence, the present research on "Parents' Opinion towards Girl Child—A Study amongst School Teachers in Tirupati" is undertaken.

Aim of the Study

The present study aims at studying the socio-economic profiles of teachers who are also parents and have daughters. They are the respondents. Further, the study also attempts to explore the opinion of the teachers about their girl child's education, health and nutritional care, social participation, psychological development, employment support and their opinion about government schemes for the welfare of girl child. Accordingly, the study has before it the following specific objectives:

Objectives of the Study

The present study has the following objectives:

1. To understand the socio-demographic and economic profile of the respondents,
2. To know the respondents' opinion about their girl child's education,
3. To know the respondents' opinion about their girl child's health and nutritional care,
4. To understand the respondents' opinion about their girl child's social participation,
5. To explore the respondents' opinion about their girl child's psychological development,
6. To know the respondents' opinion about their girl child's employment support,
7. To find out the respondents' opinion about the government welfare schemes for the betterment of the girl child,
8. To compare the respondents' opinion about their girl child's education with they type of school they are

working, the training they have undergone, the number of daughters they have and their income level,

9. To assess the effect of family income and family size on respondents' opinion about their girl child's health and nutritional care,
10. To find out the impact of the respondent's sex, religion, marital status, type of family, opinion regarding their girl child's social participation,
11. To find out the effect of the respondent's sex and education on opinion regarding their girl child's psychological development,
12. To know the effect of the type of school the respondents are working, marital status, and their opinion about their girl child's employment support,
13. To observe the influence of the respondents' sex and their income on their opinion regarding the girl child welfare schemes,
14. To identify the impact of socio-economic aspects of the respondent on their opinion regarding girl child's education, health and nutritional care, social participation, psychological development and employment support.

To verify the above objectives of the study certain hypotheses are framed and tested. They are:

Hypotheses

1. The respondents' opinion about their girl child's education is significantly influenced by the type of school they are working,
2. The respondents' opinion about their girl child's education differs according to the training they have undergone,
3. The respondents' opinion about their girl child's education is significantly influenced by the number of daughters they have,
4. The respondents' opinion about their girl child's education is dominantly influenced by their income level,

5. The respondent's opinion about their girl child's health and nutritional care is influenced by their other source of income,
6. The respondents' opinion about their girl child's health and nutritional care is significantly influenced by the size of their family,
7. The respondents' opinion about their girl child's social participation is influenced by their sex,
8. The respondents' opinion about their girl child's social participation is significantly influenced by their marital status,
9. The respondents' opinion about their girl child's social participation is dominantly influenced by their religion,
10. The respondents' opinion about their girl child's social participation is significantly influenced by the respondents' type of family.
11. The respondents' opinion about their girl child's psychological development depends upon to the type of school they are working in.
12. The respondents' opinion about their girl child's psychological status is influenced by the respondents marital status.
13. The respondents' opinion about their girl child's employment status is dominantly influenced by the type of school they are working in,
14. The respondents' opinion about their girl child's employment status is influenced by the marital status of the respondents.
15. There is a significant difference between male and female respondents' opinion about the implementation of welfare programme for girls,
16. The respondents' opinion about the importance of welfare programmes is significantly influenced by their income.

Place of the Study

Chittoor is one of the four districts comprising the region of Rayalaseema in the state of Andhra Pradesh. The other districts of the region are Kurnool, Kadapa and Ananthapur. Tirupati, where the present enquiry is carried out, belongs to Chittoor District. It is now one of the most important cities in Andhra Pradesh. Tirupati-Tirumala is famous throughout India as one of the most famous pilgrim centres, drawing several thousands of people every day who come to worship Lord Venkateswara whose temple is located on Tirumala Hills. Tirupati is located at the footsteps of Tirumala Hills. Apart from its importance as a pilgrim centre, Tirupati has other attractions. It is a premier education centre, housing half a dozen universities and a host of schools and colleges ranging from the elementary schools, post-graduate and advances research institutions. It has a number of commercial and establishments. It has an enviable number of hospitals providing medical care and health facilities. The institutions run by the Tirumala Tirupati Devasthanams employ several thousands of people. For these and other reasons Tirupati has grown to be an important urban centre in the state, and its Municipality is raised to the status of Corporation. By road, rail, and air this city is connected virtually with all parts of India. A majority of people of Tirupati have immigrated to it in recent decades from different parts of the state and elsewhere for reasons mentioned above. According to the 2001 census, the sedentary population of Tirupati is 2,53,327, covering an area of 24.07 sq. km. The present study attempts to explore the attitudes and opinions of teachers working in Elementary, Upper Primary and Higher Schools of Tirupati who are also parents, about their girl children's education, health and nutritional care, psychological development, social participation and employment support. Tirupati having become a very important education centre has a very large number of teachers coming from different backgrounds, both rural and urban who are moderately and highly educated, and whose outlook in general ranges between the tradition and modern. Thus, Tirupati provides a fertile field for the present kind of enquiry. As gathered from the Deputy Education Officer, Tirupati, Deputy Education Officer, TTD, Tirupati, Municipal Corporation, Education Officer, Tirupati, etc., the total number of school teachers working in Tirupati urban area is 4,503 (2005). Of them 1934 are men and 2,569 are women.

Universe of the Study

The universe of the study consists of teachers both men and women who working in the schools of Tirupati town. Information regarding the schools and teachers was collected from the Deputy Education Officer, Tirupati, Educational Officer of Tirupati Municipal Corporation and Tirumala Tirupati Devasthanams Education Officer etc., after explaining to them the objectives and purpose of the research work undertaken. The number of schools in Tirupati being many one had o be selective to keep the study representative and within manageable limits. From the list obtained from various educational offices a suitable number of schools were selected and visited personally to collect reliable and authentic information about the teachers who have both girl child and boy child. The data for the explorative study has collected between 2005 December to 2006 March from 4503 teachers in the town, 60 teachers from high schools, 90 teachers from upper primary schools, 150 teachers from elementary schools were selected for the study, taking the total number of respondents 300 in all.

REsearch Design

The research design is descriptive and it aims at gaining insights into the respondent, Teacher's socio-demographic and economic profile concerned. It is exploratory in certain aspects like the teachers opinion on their girl child's education, health and nutritional care, social participation, psychological development, employment support and opinion on the government welfare schemes for girls.

Sampling Design

All the schools in Tirupati are divided into 3 groups namely High schools (81), Upper primary schools (119); elementary schools (198). Then a stratified proportional random sample of 50 schools was selected. The sample consists of 10 high schools, 15 upper primary schools and 25 elementary schools.

Teachers were drawn from three groups i.e., group-1 comprises high school teachers, group-2 comprises upper primary school teachers and group-3 comprises elementary school teachers. Thus, the sample consists of 300 teachers drawn from the 50 schools selected by using stratified sampling with satisfying the condition has both boy and girl child for facilitating the respondent to give their actual opinion on the girl child.

Selection of Schools/Teachers

Schools	*High School*	*Upper Primary School*	*Elementary School*	*Total*
Universe of the study	81 (907)	119 (1349)	198 (2247)	398 (4503)
Sample of the study	10 (60)	15 (90)	25 (150)	50 (300)

Note : Figures in brackets indicates the number of Teachers.

Tools of the Study

In view of the objectives of the study, an interview schedule was framed to know the information regarding independent and dependent variables in the study. The main dependent variable in the study were respondents' opinion on their girl child's education, health and nutritional care, social participation, psychological development, employment support and their opinion on Government welfare schemes for girl child. An interview schedule was developed to collect relevant information from the respondents. The whole interview schedule is divided into three parts. Part 1 which has only one category consists of 20 questions pertaining to the socio economic and demographic information. Part 2 consists of five categories, namely 2, 3, 4, 5 and 6. Category 2, consists of 14 statements regarding the respondents' opinion about their girl child's education. Category 3, comprises 8 statements regarding the respondents' opinion about their girl child's health and nutritional care. Category 4 consists of 16 statements regarding the respondent's opinion about their girl child's social participation. Category 5 comprises 8 statements regarding the respondents' opinion about their girl child's psychological development. Category 6 consists of 8 statements regarding their girl child's employment support. Part 3 has only one category, numbered 7, and it consists of 9 statements regarding the respondents' opinion about various government welfare programmes being implemented for the betterment of the girl child.

PRE-TESTING

Before testing the main sample, the above interview schedule was administered to 50 teachers other than those in the sample for the purpose of testing the suitability of the items included in it. The interview schedule was thus found to be appropriate and would consistently measure the variables of the study.

METHOD OF DATA COLLECTION

To collect the data from the respondents, first the addresses of the selected schools were identified and the teachers. These were approached to interact with them. Next the teachers who have both a girl and a boy child were identified, and the nature and scope of the research work was explained and their consent obtained. Further, they were assured of the confidentiality of their views and opinions. Thereafter, a convenient time was fixed for the interview with the respondents. And their co-operation was sought and obtained. The interviews were conducted at the residence of the respondents or some times in the schools where the respondents are working. Thus, the convenience of the respondents was taken into consideration to conduct the interviews. Then, the interview schedule was administered to the respondents. Besides interview, observation method was also used while collecting the data pertaining to teachers' opinion about their girl child to support the information given by them. Some respondents answered the questions very spontaneously. But some others answered the questions only after each and every item in the schedule was clarified. The data was collected through personal interviews and which were mostly informal. Each interview lasted for about one and half hours.

Analysis of the Data

The data thus collected has been analyzed by using certain well established statistical techniques such as the following:

1. Percentages, mean, median, standard deviation have been calculated for a large number of variables in the study.
2. The statistical analysis is carried out with the help of the SPSS 9.0. The actual data provided by the 300 respondents was initially entered and manipulated in the SPSS Windows and advance calculations were carried out in the SPSS.
3. Comparison of mean scores with respect to respondents' opinion about their girl child's health status and welfare, sex of the respondents and type of family they belong had been made by using 't' test.
4. Comparison of respondents' mean scores about their girl child's education, health and nutritional care, social participation, psychological development, employment support and opinion about government welfare schemes in respect of their education, income, type of school, the respondent's are working, number of girls, marital status, family size, religion, etc., with the help of ANOVA (one way Analysis of Variance).
5. Stepwise regression analysis is carried out to find out the contribution of certain socio-demographic variables like education, gender, income, religion, family size, marital status, etc., to the respondents' opinion regarding their girl child's education, health and nutritional care, social participation, psychological development, employment support, and opinion about government welfare schemes for girls.

Limitation of the Study

1. The present study is conducted only in an urban area. If the study had included the rural area also, it would have

been possible to generalize about results more comprehensively.

2. The study is confined to the respondents' opinion about their girl child only. If the study had included the respondents' opinion about their boy child also, it would have been helpful to compare the results. If the study had included both parents opinions and their treatment of their girl child, it would have been possible to more accurate results regarding the girl child status, could have been arrived at and elucidated.

3. Even though, the researcher is conscious of the limitation, she has had to draw some limits to her enquiry so that it could be completed within the time permissible. It is her hope too that the conclusions arrived at the end of the study would remain valid and worthy of attention, notwithstanding the limitations.

Operational Definitions of the Major Concepts used in the Study

Teachers

'Teachers' in the study are those teachers who are working in schools in the Tirupati urban area, and have both girl and boy children.

Opinion about the Girl Child

'Opinion about the girl child' means the degree of positive or negative effect associated with the psychology of the parents.

It also means the degree of supportive or non supportive attitude associated with parents of the girl child.

Opinion about Education

In the present study, opinion about education includes, 'the respondents' views on arranging facilities for their girl child's education'.

Opinion about Health and Nutritional Care

In the present study, opinion about health and nutritional care includes 'the respondents' perceptions of the parents' role and responsibility in the health care of their girl child.

Opinion about Social Participation

In the present study opinion about social participation is understood to mean 'the respondents' attitudes towards or views on providing social training to their girl children'.

Opinion about Psychological Development

In the study, the opinion about psychological development means the parent's perceptions on their support to their girl child in her personality development.

Opinion about Employment Support

Opinions about employment support means in the study "the scope or provision given to the girl child by her parents to get a suitable employment'.

SCHEME OF CHAPTERIZATION

The thesis is divided into 5 chapters. Chapter-I is introductory and it discusses aspects related to the status of the girl child and her problems, and the available legal, welfare support to her. Chapter-II covers a review of relevant literature, Chapter -III deals with research methodology adopted in the study. It also spells out in clearer terms the theme of investigation, its scope and objectives and its limitations. Chapter-IV deals with the findings of the enquiry followed by a discussion. Chapter-V presents a summary of the study, conclusions drawn, and viable suggestions to better the lot of the girl child.

4

Results and Discussion

Opinion of teachers regarding the girl child is extremely important as they are the chief source of knowledge for pupils in their early stages of education. The teacher, outside home, exerts the greatest influence on his/her pupils. Most young and growing minds look their teachers at school for guidance, and unconsciously shape themselves after them. Therefore, a great responsibility rests on their shoulders, and try, their level best to inculcate and moral social, ethical values in their students. The teacher's life, opinions, attitudes, values and outlook make a lasting impression on the students. And hence, he or she can play a decisive role in bringing about desirable attitudinal changes in their pupils regarding the girl child. As Corson (1993) puts it, "gender attitudes may be isolated and gender bias can be corrected through promoting school based action".

In the previous chapter attempt has been made to state clearly the problems of inquiry, its significance, its range and scope as well its limits and limitations. This chapter also explains the sample chosen, the methodology adopted, variables and the hypotheses to be tested and verified.

This chapter explains the socio-economic and demographic information of the respondents, their opinions about their girl child's education, health and nutritional care, social participation, psychological development, employment support and their opinion regarding government welfare schemes for girls. The data collected systematically is analysed and presented in the form of tables with percentages and statistical analysis. The statistical analysis enables the researcher to arrive at scientific and meaningful conclusions. The analysed data is presented in the following tables.

Socio-Economic and Demographic Status

Table 1
Socio-Demographic Information of the Sample in the Present Study

S.No.	*Sub Group*	*No.*	*Percentage*
1.	Gender		
	Male	150	50.0
	Female	150	50.0
	Total	300	100
2.	Age		
	Upto 30 years	093	31.0
	30-40 years	110	36.7
	40-50 years	059	19.7
	Above 50 years	038	12.7
	Total	300	100
3.	Religion		
	Hindu	234	78.0
	Muslim	024	08.0
	Christian	033	11.0
	Others, specify	009	03.0
	Total	300	100
4.	Caste		
	Forward Caste	161	53.7
	Other Backward Castes	091	30.3
	Scheduled Castes	040	13.3
	Scheduled Tribes	008	02.7
	Total	300	100
5.	Marital Status		
	Married	272	90.7
	Divorced/separated	008	02.7
	Widow/Widower	018	06.0
	Unmarried	002	00.7
	Total	300	100

Sex differentiation is a fact of life from which two distinct sets of roles, statuses and societal groups emerge. Since the study is an attempt to know the opinion of teachers about the girl child, it is essential to include in it both men and women teachers to elicit accurate information on their opinions of the girl child.

As is clear from Table 1, the sample of respondents consists of an equal percentage of men and women (50% each). Generally with age one grows mature intellectually and economically. Such maturity of mind and heart is very essential for a teacher, whether man or woman, while imparting knowledge to their pupils. In the process of teaching eager pupils, thoughts and ideas, such as for example the importance of the girl child, her role and status in the family and society, the prevailing attitudes towards all girl children and the urgent need to bring about an attitudinal change regarding all girl children for the better yet clarified. Thus, the teacher can make an indelible impression on the young and growing minds and help them to develop right opinions and attitudes. Therefore, the age of the respondents has been studied in the present study. Further, it implies the extent of their maturity and understanding of the status of girl child. Table 1 shows that 36.7 per cent of the teachers belong to the age group of 30-40 years, followed by 31.0 per cent who belongs to 'upto 30 years age group', 19.7 per cent to 40-50 years age group and 12.7 per cent belong to above 50 years age group.

India is a land of several religious, and therefore people have various religious backgrounds and follow various customs and traditions, which mould their attitudes and life-styles. Knowing the respondents' social background in respect of their religion etc., would probably help was to understand their social outlook especially their opinion of the girl child, etc. It may be observed from Table 1 that a majority (i.e., 78 per cent) of the respondents are Hindus followed by 11 per cent who are Christians and 8 per cent Muslims and 3 per cent to other religions i.e., Jains.

The centuries old caste system is used as the criterion by the Central and Governments to initiate schemes/programmes for the girl child and distribute the benefits among girl children. Table 1 reveals that, a majority of the respondents, that is 53.7 per cent, belong to the 'forward caste' category (Kamma and Reddy) followed by 30.3 per cent who belong to 'other backward castes', 13.3 per cent to the Scheduled Castes and 2.7 per cent belong to the Scheduled Tribes.

Table 2
Socio-Demographic Information of the Sample in the Present Study

S.No.	*Sub Group*	*No.*	*Percentage*
1.	Family Type		
	Joint	087	29.0
	Nuclear	213	71.0
	Total	300	100
2.	Size of Family		
	1-3	014	04.7
	4-6	216	72.0
	7-9	051	17.0
	9 and above	019	06.3
	Total	300	100
3.	Number of Daughters		
	1	179	59.7
	2	090	30.0
	3	024	08.0
	4 and above	007	02.3
	Total	300	100
4.	Number of Sons		
	1	244	81.3
	2	039	13.0
	3	015	05.0
	4 and above	002	00.7
	Total	300	100
5.	Type of School (Government/Private)		
	Government school	051	17.0
	Government aided school	177	59.0
	Private school	072	24.0
	Total	300	100
6.	School of Working		
	Elementary school	150	50.0
	Upper primary school	090	30.0
	High school	060	20.0
	Total	300	100

The Marital status of the respondents is an important factor influencing their opinion of the girl child's status. It is evident from Table 1 that, the majority (i.e., 90.7 per cent) of the respondents are married and the spouses live together. The table also makes clear in what sense the term 'Marital status' is used in the study.

Families in India traditionally were generally 'joint' as land was the common source of income and fathers and sons with their wives and children lived together. With the advent of technology, industrialization and urbanization, the joint family system has yielded place to the nuclear family system. Still in Indian villages, the joint family system is widely prevalent. Type of family influences the opinions and attitudes of people regarding various issue including the girl child issue. Hence, an effect is made to know the exact influence of the type of family on the respondents regarding on this issue.

It is clear from Table 2 that, a majority (i.e., 71 per cent) of the respondents live in nuclear families and the remaining 29 per cent of the respondents live in joint families.

Information on family size indicates the extent of pressure the family size exerts on its resource, and it also refers to the family status. "An average rural family prefers sons for support in their old age which contributes to a bigger family size" (Sisodia, 2003). Table 2 reveals that, nearly three-fourths of the respondents families (72 per cent) consist of 4 to 6 members, while 17 per cent of the families have 7 to 9 persons and 6.3 per cent of families have 9 and above members. In general, most of the people do not wish to have many daughters. If a couple have more daughters, it is due to their desire for a male issue or they are waiting to have a son.

It is noticed from Table 2 that, 59.7 per cent of the respondents have one daughter while 30 per cent of the respondents are have two daughters, 8 per cent three daughters, and 2.3 per cent have daughters 4 and more. "Each successive girl in the family is less welcome than the earlier one" (Karkal, 1999). The composition of children in a family especially the number of sons has much to do with the expectation of parents. There is a common belief that sons are 'the redeemers of parents from hell'. Further, having more sons is a matter of privilege and prestige to the parents in society. Table 2 shows that, 81.3 per cent of the respondents have one son and 13 per cent respondents have two sons.

The details of the number of girls and of boys reveal that among the respondents 31 (24 + 7) have 3 and more than 3 daughters, whereas 17 (15 + 2) respondents have 3 and more sons. These figures clearly show that the respondents gave birth to more girl children while waiting for a boy child.

The place of work of the respondents, whether in the government sector or private sector may have a significant influence on their opinions and decisions regarding their life events. Because the job one has is not only a source of income but it is his/her security. So, it has much influence on an individual's opinions. Table 2 reveals that, 59 per cent of the respondents are working in Government-aided schools and 24 per cent are working in private schools. Table 2 also gives the details of schools in which the respondents are working, 50 per cent of them are working in elementary schools, 30 per cent working in upper primary schools, and 20 per cent are working in high schools.

Education is one of the basic indicators of socio-economic characteristics. The Educational background of an individual determines several aspects of his day-to-day life.

From Table 3, it is clear that, more than half of the respondents (56.3 per cent) are graduates and 19 per cent post-graduates. Not only education, be it graduate or post-graduate is essential for all school teachers. Educational level forms an important basis for differentiating between individuals, besides deciding their social status. It builds one's capacity to resolve personal and interpersonal problems and influences their opinions and role performance. Qualified and trained teachers are very essential for providing quality education. If teachers are well qualified and dedicated to the cause, then the rate of dropouts especially that of girl children can be reduced. Training of teachers is crucial for qualitative improvement in education. It will equip them with skills necessary for inculcating interest in young minds for education and, thereby, strengthening the education system. Table 3 shows that 61.3

per cent of the respondents have undergone B.Ed. training, 16.7 per cent teacher training (DIET) and 8.3 per cent M.Ed. training, 4.3 per cent technical trainings like drawing, music, etc., and a less 9.3 per cent have undergone B.P.Ed. training.

Table 3

Education and Economic Information of the Sample in the Present Study

S.No.	Sub Group	No.	Percentage
1.	Education		
	Intermediate	049	16.3
	Graduation	169	56.3
	Post-graduation	057	19.0
	Ph.D.	007	02.3
	Pandit and technical courses	018	06.0
	Total	300	100
2.	Training undergone		
	Teacher training	050	16.7
	B.Ed.	184	61.3
	M.Ed.	025	08.3
	Technical training	013	04.3
	B.P.Ed., etc.	028	09.3
	Total	300	100
3.	Income of Respondents		
	Upto Rs. 3000	049	16.3
	Rs. 3001-6000	061	20.3
	Rs. 6001-9000	092	30.7
	Rs. 9001-12000	067	22.3
	Rs. 12001 and above	031	10.3
	Total	300	100
4.	Family Income		
	Rs. 5000	039	13.0
	Rs. 5001-10000	105	35.0
	Rs. 10001-15000	081	27.0
	Rs. 15001 and above	075	25.0
	Total	300	100
5.	Other sources of Income		
	No other source (other than spouse)	114	38.0
	House rent	042	14.0
	Agriculture and allied sources	040	13.3
	Interests and returns on savings, etc.	037	12.3
	Business	030	10.0
	Children, etc.	037	12.3
	Total	300	100

Adequate income is the single most important determinant of the wellbeing of persons at any stage of the life cycle. It reflects their economic condition and capacity to avail themselves of services. It is also crucial to their decision-making on various issues in life. Table 3 shows that a little more than one-fourth of the respondents (30.7 per cent) belong to the income group of Rs. 6001-9000 per month. They are followed by 22.3 per cent of respondents who belong to the Rs. 9,001 to 12,000 group, 20.3 per cent to the Rs. 3,001-6,000 income group, 16.3 per cent to the income group of Rs. 3000 and below and only 10.3 per cent belong to the Rs. 12,001 and above income group.

The economic conditions of the parents or family would be the most significant factor in girls pursuing education than getting sufficient nutrition and guidance for employment also determine the parents' taking decisions regarding their children. Further, the family income also influcnces the parents' choice into make arrangements for the needs of their children. Table 3 reveals that the monthly family income of 35 per cent of the respondents is between Rs. 5,001 and 10,000, of 27 per cent between Rs. 10,001 and 15,000, of 25 per cent is Rs. 15,001 and above, and of 13 per cent below Rs. 5,000 per month.

Now-a-days one is not able to meet his/her needs with only one source of income because of ever increasing cost of living. So every one makes some arrangements to get additional income through durable assets, savings, business, agriculture, etc. Having an additional income has become a pre-requisite to combat the expenditure of the everyday needs of the family. Table 3 shows that among the respondents, 38 per cent do not have any other source of income than their monthly salary. Among those who have other sources of income, 14 per cent are getting income through house rent, 13.3 per cent from agriculture and allied sources etc., 12.3 per cent from interest and returns on savings and from children, and 10 per cent get additional income from business.

Money savings are very important in one's life as they facilitate individuals to face the challenges of unexpected expenditure of the family either at present or in future. It is clear from Table 4 that the majority (82 per cent) of the respondents have some savings. Among them, 48 per cent save less than Rs. 1000 per month, 23 per cent Rs. 1001-2000, 13.3 per cent save Rs. 2001 and above per month. This clearly indicates that most of the respondents have the savings habit and that they have the ability to take care of their children's needs effectively.

The economic condition of the parents would be the most decisive factor in enrolling their children in schools, arranging nutritious food, for them, for their proper health care, etc. Several studies of the girl child have identified poverty (lack of adequate economic resources) for persistent child labor, dropping out from school, etc. The ever-increasing cost of living comes in the way of fulfilling the family needs. It is clear from Table 4 that a little more than half of the respondents (54.3%) state that their economic sources are partly adequate, 27 per cent state that they are completely sufficient, 18.7 per cent state that their economic sources are not at all sufficient to meet the family expenditure.

Most employees usually manage their planned, unplanned or unexpected expenditures through raising loans from banks or from their offices. In some cases, they go to money-lenders or others to get loans.

Table 4 also gives details of financial management of the respondents when faced with a financial crisis or emergency. 29.3 per cent of the respondents manage the financial emergencies by raising loans from banks or from their own office, 17.7 per cent by getting loans from money-lenders, 15.7 per cent by getting loans from friends and relatives, and 10.3 per cent depend on their own savings.

Generally, most people go for loans for purposes like childrens' education, employment, marriage, health, other family expenditure or to start some business for their children. Table 4 reveals the details of the purposes for which loans taken by the respondents. And it is noticed that only 18 per cent raised loans for their sons' education, employment and business, 16.7 per cent for their family expenditure, 16 per cent for their daughters' education, employment and business, and 11.3 per cent exclusively for the purpose of their daughter's marriage.

Table 4
Economic Information of the Sample in the Present Study

S.No.	*Sub Group*	*No.*	*Percentage*
1.	Savings		
	Yes	246	82.0
	No	054	18.0
	Total	300	100
2.	Saving amount per month		
	Less than Rs. 1000	144	48.0
	Rs. 1001-2000	069	23.0
	Rs. 2001 and above	040	13.3
	Not applicable	047	15.7
	Total	300	100.0
3.	Sufficiency of economic sources		
	Not at al	056	18.7
	Partly	163	54.3
	Completely	081	27.0
	Total	300	100
4.	Management of financial crisis		
	Loans from banks and office	088	29.3
	Loans from money lenders	053	17.7
	Loans from friends and relatives	047	15.7
	Using savings, etc.	031	10.3
	Not applicable	081	27.0
	Total	300	100
5.	Purposes of loans taken		
	Son's education, employment and business	048	16.0
	Daughter's education, employment & business	054	18.0
	Daughter's marriage	034	11.3
	Health of the family	033	11.0
	Family expenditure	050	16.7
	Not applicable	081	27.0
	Total	300	100
6.	Duration of repayment		
	Monthly	080	26.7
	Half yearly	055	18.3
	Yearly	030	10.0
	Whenever possible	054	18.0
	Not applicable	081	27.0
	Total	300	100

From Table 4 it may be known the duration of repayment of loans by the respondents. 26.7 per cent are repaying the loans in monthly installments. 18.3 per cent half-yearly installments and 18 per cent respondents repay the loans whenever there is possibility for them to repay the loan.

Respondents' Opinion about Their Girl Child's Education

Table 5
Distribution of Respondents According to Their Opinion on the Importance of Education for their Girl Children

S.No.	*Education is Important for Girl Child*	*Number*	*Percentage*
1.	Strongly Disagree	016	05.3
2.	Disagree	017	05.7
3.	Agree	187	62.3
4.	Strongly Agree	080	26.7
	Total	300	100

Education for girls is a crucial input for preserving and developing their resources mental, moral, spiritual, so that they can enjoy the fruits of social justice, social, cultural, political and economic rights. It is clear from Table 6 that, a majority i.e., 62.3 per cent of the respondents 'agree' that education is important for girls, followed by 26.7 per cent of respondents who 'strongly agree' and 11 per cent (5.7 + 5.3) disagree with the view that education is important for girls. Further, the parents' educational status also influences their opinion of education and welfare of the children, especially the girl child.

From Table 6, it is noticed that more than half of the respondents (58.3 per cent) 'agreed' that 'parents can reduce girls dropping out of school. 20.7 per cent of the respondents 'strongly agree', with this view, 13.3 per cent disagree with it, and a very small percentage of them (7.7 per cent) strongly disagree with this views. Socialization of girl children and decisions regarding them, especially girl's education is the responsibility of parents. If the parents are well qualified and dedicated to the cause, then the problems of 'girl child dropping out' would be reduced.

Table 6
Distribution of Respondents according to Their Opinion about Parents Role to Reduce School Dropouts among Girl Children

S.No.	*Parents can Reduce School Dropouts among Girl Children*	*Number*	*Percentage*
1.	Strongly Disagree	023	07.7
2.	Disagree	040	13.3
3.	Agree	175	58.3
4.	Strongly Agree	062	20.7
	Total	300	100

Table 7
Distribution of Respondents according to Their Opinion of Minimum Education for Girl Child

S.No.	*Minimum Education (Inter, Graduation) is not enough for Girl Child*	*Number*	*Percentage*
1.	Strongly Disagree	025	08.3
2.	Disagree	064	21.3
3.	Agree	172	57.3
4.	Strongly Agree	039	13.0
	Total	300	100

From Table 7, it is observed that 57.3 per cent of the respondents 'agree' with the statement that education upto inter and graduation is not enough for girls, 13 per cent 'strongly agree' with this view, whereas 29.6 per cent (21.3 + 8.3) 'disagree' and 'strongly disagree' with it. There seem to be more than one reason for holding the view that education beyond degree is not necessary for girls. It may be due to the fact educating a girl is expensive and an indirect loss of earning. It may lead to shortage of man-power for performing household work. Further, it is expected that girls will have to marry at a young age and join their husbands' families. Therefore, those parents do not prefer to provide higher education to their daughters.

Table 8
Distribution of Respondents according to Their Opinion of Professional Education for Girl Child

S.No.	*Professional Education is Necessary*	*Number*	*Percentage*
1.	Strongly Disagree	017	05.7
2.	Disagree	120	40.0
3.	Agree	149	49.7
4.	Strongly Agree	014	04.7
	Total	300	100

Table 8 explains that, very nearly half of the respondents (49.7%) 'agree' that professional education is necessary for girls, but 40 per cent 'disagree' with this view. And 5.7% of them can strongly disagree. Now-a-days many women who are graduates in non-professional subjects are getting employed and earning adequate income. Further, professional education is far more expensive than non-professional education so that many parents do not favour professional courses for their girl children. There could be other reasons too. Have you considered those possibilities! For instance, education in engineering, medicine and such courses may require girls to go to far away from home. Many parents may hesitate to send their daughters to such distant places.

Table 9
Distribution of Respondents according to Their Opinion of Government School Education for Girl Children

S.No.	*Government School Education is not Enough for Girl Child*	*Number*	*Percentage*
1.	Strongly Disagree	049	16.3
2.	Disagree	131	43.7
3.	Agree	085	28.3
4.	Strongly Agree	035	11.7
	Total	300	100

It is clear from Table 9 that, 43.7 per cent of the respondents 'disagree' with the view that government school education is not enough for girl children and 28.3 per cent 'agree' to the contrary. Disagreeing with the view may be due to the fact that these respondents are at present working in government, government-aided and private schools. They hold the view that most government schools provide good education. They also feel that much depends on students and how they concentrate on education.

Table 10
Distribution of Respondents according to Their Opinion of Paying High Donation as Investment on Girl Child's Education

Respondents' Opinion	*School Education*		*College Education*		*Professional*	
	No.	*%*	*No.*	*%*	*No.*	*%*
Strongly Disagree	020	06.7	019	06.3	055	01.7
Disagree	166	55.3	165	55.0	103	34.3
Agree	108	36.0	113	37.7	172	57.3
Strongly Agree	006	02.0	003	01.0	020	06.7
Total	300	100	300	100	300	100

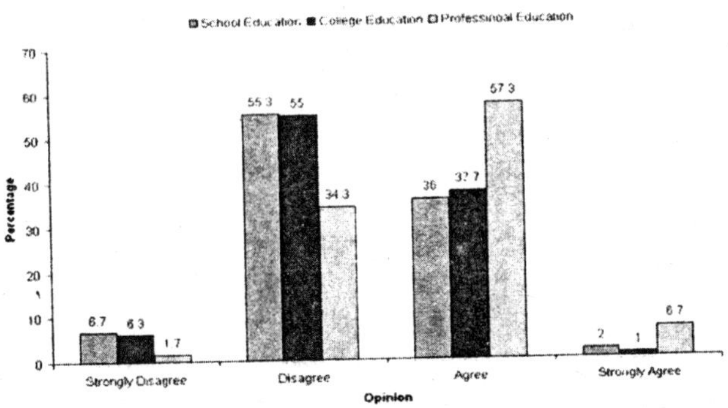

Figure 1. Opinion of Paying High Donation on Girl Child's Education

Donations are demanded by private schools. Table 10 reveals that more than half of the respondents (57.3 per cent) express their willingness (Agree) to pay huge sum of money as donations for professional courses for girls. But 55.3 per cent of the respondents are unwilling (Disagree) to pay donations for 'girls' school and college education probably because opportunities are readily available for girls' education in government schools and college. But if the children are able to get admission into professional courses and there is need to pay donations, 57.3 per cent respondents are willing to invest the amount in view of the girls possible bright future (Fig. 1).

Bhogle (1999) has observed in her study that the major discrimination is in the areas of sending the children to school, choice of school, etc. The parents are willing to send their sons to expensive schools but not their girls, because boys are after all 'ours', while the girls are 'somebody's property'.

Table 11
Distribution of Respondents according to Their Opinion of Investment of Donations on Girl Child's Education in Professional Courses Outside the State

S.No.	*Paying Donations to Professional Courses Outside the State*	*Number*	*Percentage*
1.	Strongly Disagree	026	08.7
2.	Disagree	125	41.7
3.	Agree	111	37.0
4.	Strongly Agree	038	12.7
	Total	300	100

It is clear from Table 11 that 41.7 per cent of the respondents are unwilling (Disagree) to pay donations to professional courses for their girls outside the state, while 37.0 per cent are willing (agree). 12.7 per cent are strongly agree (willing) to pay donations for their girl child's professional education and a less 8.7 per cent strongly disagree to pay donations for their girl child's professional education. Which clearly shows that though the parents are willing to pay donations for professional courses for girls within the state, they did not show much interest to invest on girls to join in professional courses from outside the state.

Table 12
Distribution of Respondents according to Their Opinion about the Necessity of Private School Education for Girl Child

S.No.	*Necessity for Private School Education for Girls*	*Number*	*Percentage*
1.	Strongly Disagree	004	01.3
2.	Disagree	128	42.7
3.	Agree	146	48.7
4.	Strongly Agree	022	7.3
	Total	300	100

It is noticed from Table 12 that, 48.7 per cent of the respondents favour the view and 'agree' that the private school education is necessary for girls and 42.7 per cent of the respondents do not approve of it. This more or less equally divided opinion among the respondents is due to the belief that innovative and quality education is available in private and government schools alike. Most of the respondents had their education in government schools and some of them are working in them at present.

Table 13
Distribution of Respondents according to Their Opinion of Parents' Help in Their Girl Child's Education

S.No.	*Parents must Help in Education of Girls*	*Number*	*Percentage*
1.	Strongly Disagree	001	00.3
2.	Disagree	016	05.3
3.	Agree	199	66.3
4.	Strongly Agree	084	28.0
	Total	300	100

It is noticed from Table 13 that, 199 or 66.3 per cent of the respondents 'agree' that parents must help in the education of girls, and 84 or 28 per cent 'strongly agree' with the view. This clearly shows that in different degrees the majority of the respondents feel that parents must take the responsibility of educating of their girl children. The respondents being both teachers and parents their support to the view that parents must be responsible for girl chlidren's education is really significant.

Table 14

Distribution of Respondents according to Their Opinion of Arranging Private Tuitions for Girl Child

S.No.	*Private Tuitions must be Arranged for Girls*	*Number*	*Percentage*
1.	Strongly Disagree	002	00.7
2.	Disagree	156	52.0
3.	Agree	130	43.3
4.	Strongly Agree	012	04.0
	Total	300	100

It is observed from the Table 14, that a little more than half of the respondents (52 per cent) 'disagree' on private tuitions to be arranged for girls but 43.3 per cent 'agree' on it. Obviously a majority of the respondents do not approve of private tuitions for girls to improve their education and performance.

Table 15

Distribution of Respondents according to Their Opinion about Government Help by Reservation, Free Education, etc., for Girl Child

S.No.	*Reservation, Free Education etc., Help Girl Child*	*Number*	*Percentage*
1.	Strongly Disagree	001	00.3
2.	Disagree	024	08.0
3.	Agree	171	57.0
4.	Strongly Agree	104	34.7
	Total	300	100

It is clear from Table 15 that, a majority (57.0 per cent) of the respondents 'agree' that reservation, free education and such programmes help girls to acquire education, and 34.7 per cent of the respondents 'strongly agree' with this view. This clearly shows that reservation, free education and other privileges like appointment of female teachers, setting up of separate schools for girls are essential. It is not accidental that 275 respondents in all are in favour of extending these facilities to girl children.

Table 16
Distribution of Respondents according to Their Opinion of the Importance of Study Tours for Girl Child

S.No.	Study Tours are Essential for Recreation and Knowledge	Number	Percentage
1.	Strongly Disagree	019	06.3
2.	Disagree	136	45.3
3.	Agree	125	41.7
4.	Strongly Agree	020	06.7
	Total	300	100

It is noticed from Table 16 that, 136 (45.3 per cent) respondents 'disagree' with the view that study tours are essential for girls for their recreation and acquisition of knowledge whereas 41.7 per cent are in favour of them. It may be noticed that a little less than half of the respondents 48.4 (41.7 + 6.7) are in favour of study tour etc., while 51.6 (45.3 + 6.3) do not favour the idea that is, a little more than half of the respondents are against them.

Respondents Opinion of Their Girl Child's Health and Nutritional Care

Growth and physical development of infants and children are widely used as indicators of the overall health and nutrition status of a community and Nation.

According to Jayasree (2000) denial of nutritious food and absence of provision of health care for girls are related to traditional beliefs and practices. If the girl child is neglected and systematically deprived of care and love, and it has an impact on her physical, psychological health.

Table 17
Distribution of the Respondents according to Their Opinion of Parents' Role in Girl's Health Care

S.No.	*Parents Play Important Role in Girls Health Care*	*Number*	*Percentage*
1.	Strongly Disagree	–	–
2.	Disagree	002	00.7
3.	Agree	161	53.7
4.	Strongly Agree	137	45.7
	Total	300	100

It is clear from Table 17 that the vast majority of 99.3 per cent (161 + 137) the respondents 'agree' that parents play an important role in girls health. Only 2 or 00.7 per cent of the respondents do not accept the view.

The study results of Mittal (1991) reveal that the baby girls are subtly weaned away from breast milk much earlier than boys and they receive even less of weaning food. Further, this study reveals that the intake of 13-16 year old girls in rural India is even less than 213 of the recommended calorie intake. A welcome change is also observed in the scenario of health, as the NFHS-II (1998-98) data revealed that "there is no much difference between male and female children according to nutritional status".

Table 18
Distribution of Respondents according to Their Opinion of Necessity of Health Checkup for Girl Child

S.No.	*Regular Health Checkups are Necessary for Girls*	*Number*	*Percentage*
1.	Strongly Disagree	019	06.3
2.	Disagree	184	61.3
3.	Agree	088	29.3
4.	Strongly Agree	009	03.0
	Total	300	100

It is clear from Table 18 that, a majority (61.3 per cent) of the respondents 'disagree' that regular health checkups are necessary for girls. A small percentage of the respondents (6.3) strongly disagree of it. But 29.3 per cent 'agree' that regular health checkups are necessary. A very small percentage (3%) strongly favour regular checkups. It is rather strange that 203 respondents or 67.6% or two-thirds, teachers (who are both teachers and parents) should not favour regular health checkups for girl children. Possibly, some hesitation and vague fears and neglect to visit the doctor regularly may be responsible for viewing regular checkups as unnecessary there could also be some undefined cultural belief and gender discrimination influencing their view.

Table 19
Distribution of Respondents according to Their Opinion of the Necessity of Early Treatment of Girl Child During Illness

S.No.	*Early Treatment of Health Problems of Girl Child is Essential*	*Number*	*Percentage*
1.	Strongly Disagree	-	-
2.	Disagree	049	16.3
3.	Agree	209	69.7
4.	Strongly Agree	042	14.0
	Total	300	100

Table 19 shows that, a good majority of the respondents (69.7 per cent) agree that early treatment of health problems of their girl child is essential followed by 16.3 per cent disagree with that, and a less 14 per cent of the respondents strongly agree for early treatment of health problems of their girl child. As educated parents they are well aware of the necessity of early treatment of the health problems of their child, so that she can be physically and mentally sound.

It is noticed from Table 20 that, 48.3 per cent or 145 of the respondents 'disagree' with the view that home remedies are enough for the treatment of a girl child during illness, while 35.3 per cent or 106 respondents 'agree' with the view. It is clear from this that a majority of the parents are not in favour of home remedies for curving the health problems of their girl children. However, a small percentage of parents (10%) believe in the use of home and think that it is unnecessary to go to hospital for treatment.

Table 20
Distribution of the Respondents according to Their Opinion of Home Remedies for Girl Child

S.No.	Home Remedies are Enough for the Treatment of Girl Child	Number	Percentage
1.	Strongly Disagree	019	06.3
2.	Disagree	145	48.3
3.	Agree	106	35.3
4.	Strongly Agree	030	10.0
	Total	300	100

It is clear from Table 21 that, the majority of respondents (234 + 31) 'agree' that hospital treatment must be provided to girls though, this view contradicts the results of the studies of Karkal (1999) and Jayasree (2000). Studies in Jay Prakash Naraya Hospital, reveal that malnutrition, diarrhoea etc., are very common in girls, but while most males affected by them are hospitalized frequently, females are brought when it is too late. As a result, a proportionately there is a higher rate of mortality among them.

Table 21
Distribution of Respondents according to their Opinion of Hospital Treatment for Girls

S.No.	Hospital Treatment must be Provided for Girl Child	Number	Percentage
1.	Strongly Disagree	002	00.7
2.	Disagree	033	11.0
3.	Agree	234	78.0
4.	Strongly Agree	031	10.3
	Total	300	100

Table 22 makes it clear that, a great majority (89 per cent) of the respondents favour nutritious diet for girls and want that it must be provided. Regarding additional diet, only 56.7 per cent 'agree' that additional diet like fruits, salads, etc., should be provided to the girl child.

Table 22
Distribution of Respondents according to Their Opinion of Girl Child's Nutritious and Additional Diet

	Nutritional Diet must be Provided for Girl Child		*Additional Diet must be Provided to Girl Child*	
Respondents Opinion	*No.*	*%*	*No.*	*%*
Strongly Disagree	001	00.3	005	01.7
Disagree	013	04.3	112	37.3
Agree	267	89.0	170	56.7
Strongly Agree	019	06.3	017	04.3
Total	300	100	300	100

However, Karkal (1999) observes that, there was no discrimination between girls and boys in the amount of cereals consumed, while there was a marked difference with regard to milk and milk products, egg, ghee, non-vegetarian and other items. Mothers and girl child ate last, when at times even the basic food was not enough for them. Studies show that, there was an attempt to feed girls less in order to delay their menarche.

According to the NFHS-II data (1998-99) there is not much difference between male and female child in their nutritional status. Further, the survey observed that gender differentials exist in the lower strata of society. The respondents of the present study are all educated, working as teachers and earning a meaningful income. And hence a majority of them support the view that girl children must be provided with good and nutritious food along with additional diet which is very essential for the female child.

It is clear from Table 23 that, a majority of the respondents (i.e., 53 per cent) are not in favour of giving pocket money to girls to purchase eatables along with other expenditure. But only 21.3 per cent agree with the view, 13 per cent of the respondents were strongly agree for that and a less 12.7 per cent strongly disagree to giving pocket money to girl child. Similar results were observed by Ghosh (1995) in his study. He says: "boys ate more raw vegetables, fruits and eatables when they were out of the house and had some pocket money for school as well. But girls are denied these extras". In the present study more than half of the respondents are against pocket money to girls probably because they think that pocket money may spoil the girls and then purchasing eatables outside home is not good for health, etc.

Table 23
Distribution of Respondents according to Their Opinion of Giving Pocket Money to Girl Child

S.No.	*Pocket Money must be given to Girls to Purchase Eatables*	*Number*	*Percentage*
1.	Strongly Disagree	038	12.7
2.	Disagree	159	53.0
3.	Agree	064	21.3
4.	Strongly Agree	039	13.0
	Total	300	100

Respondent's Opinion of Their Girl Child's Social Participation

Table 24
Distribution of Respondents according to Their Opinion of Their Girl Child's Participation in Sports and Indoor Games

S.No.	*Girl Child must Participate in Sports/Indoor Games*	*Spots*		*Indoor Games*	
		No.	*Percentage*	*No.*	*Percentage*
1.	Strongly Disagree	002	00.7	003	01.0
2.	Disagree	018	06.0	069	23.0
3.	Agree	171	57.0	166	55.3
4.	Strongly Agree	108	36.3	062	20.7
	Total	300	100	300	100

As Table 24 shows, 57 per cent of the respondents (171) 'agree' that girls must participate in outdoor sports, and 36.3 per cent (108) strongly advocate it.. Regarding indoor games also a majority of 55.3 per cent of respondents 'agree' that girl child must participate in indoor games and 20.7 per cent more 'strongly agree' with the view. Obviously, most of the parents expect their girl child to participate in sports and indoor games, etc. They believe that for both physical and psychological development of children games and sports are very useful.

It is revealed from Table 25 that, 63 per cent of the respondents (189) 'disagree' that the girl child needs training in dance and music whereas 25.3 per cent (76) 'agree' with the idea. Among the respondents, 120 (40 per cent) 'disagree' with the idea that girl child needs training in martial arts. However, one group of 76 of the respondents another 44 respondents 'agree' and 'strongly agree' respectively with the view that girls must be given training in martial arts. This clearly shows that more parents of girl children favour providing training in martial arts than dance and music, probably because they feel that girls should know how to protect themselves.

Table 25
Distribution of Respondents According to Their Opinion about the Need of Training in Dance, Music and Martial Arts for Girl Child

S.No.	*Girl Child Need Training in Dance, Music and Martial Arts*	*Dance and Music*		*Martial Arts*	
		No.	*Percentage*	*No.*	*Percentage*
1.	Strongly Disagree	017	05.7	029	09.7
2.	Disagree	189	63.0	120	40.0
3.	Agree	076	25.3	107	35.7
4.	Strongly Agree	018	06.0	044	14.7
	Total	300	100	300	100

It is clear from Table 26 that 113 or 37.7 per cent of the respondents 'agree' that girl child must participate in competitions in local places, but 101 or 33.7 per cent of respondents 'disagree' with that view. Further, it is noticed that 136 or 45.3 per cent of the respondents 'agree' that girls must participate in competition in outstation places followed. But 84 or 28 per cent of the respondents 'disagree' with that view. The figures show that among the respondents more people (163 and 183) are in favour of their girl children participating in competitions held locally and in outstation places.

Table 26
Distribution of Respondents according to Their Opinion about Participation of Girl Child in Competitions in Local and Outstation Places

S.No.	*Girl Child must Participate in Competitions*	*Local Places*		*Outstation Places*	
		No.	*Percentage*	*No.*	*Percentage*
1.	Strongly Disagree	036	12.0	033	11.0
2.	Disagree	101	33.7	084	28.0
3.	Agree	113	37.7	136	45.3
4.	Strongly Agree	050	16.7	047	15.7
	Total	300	100	300	100

Table 27
Distribution of Respondents according to their Opinion about the Need of Separate Schools for Girl Children

S.No.	*The No Need of Separate Schools for Girl Children*	*Number*	*Percentage*
1.	Strongly Disagree	030	10.0
2.	Disagree	180	60.0
3.	Agree	041	13.7
4.	Strongly Agree	049	16.3
	Total	300	100

It is clear from Table 27 that a majority of the respondents (60 per cent) 'disagree' with the statement that there is no need for separate schools for girls, but 16.3 per cent favour separate schools for them. Actually, the table shows that 210 (30 + 180) respondents (10% + 60%) favour for separate schools for girls. But only 90 (41 + 49) respondents do not favour separate schools for girls.

Table 28
Distribution of Respondents according to their Opinion about Training for Girl Child in Housekeeping and Marketing Only

S.No.	*Training should be provided for Girl Child only in House-keeping and Marketing*	*House Keeping*		*Marketing etc.*	
		No.	*Percentage*	*No.*	*Percentage*
1.	Strongly Disagree	016	05.3	019	06.3
2.	Disagree	058	19.3	057	19.0
3.	Agree	184	61.3	187	62.3
4.	Strongly Agree	042	14.0	037	12.3
	Total	300	100	300	100

It is clear from Table 28 that, 61.3 per cent of the respondents 'agree' that training should be provided to girl child in house-keeping, while 19.3 per cent 'disagree' with that view. These respondents though educated and employed, seem to view that house-keeping is female responsibility and therefore girl children only should be given training in house-keeping. Further, regarding marketing, the results reveal that a majority i.e., 62.3 per cent of the respondents 'agree' that the girl child needs training in marketing, payment of various bills and shopping, etc. It clearly shows that the respondents are willing to train their girl children in roles which are generally assigned to boys. Obviously these parents desire to equip their girl children with the above skills to face the present society's demands, and learn to be self-reliant.

It is noticed from Table 29 that, in all 231 of the respondents (66.3% + 10.7%) 'agree' and 'strongly agree' that girls should be married only after then attaining legal age. The legal age for girls for marriage is 18 years because then physical and psychological development will take place only after this age. The figures establish that the majority of the respondents are aware of their responsibility as parents regarding their girl children.

Table 29
Distribution of Respondents according to Their Opinion that Girl Child should be Married after attaining of Legal Age

S.No.	*Girl Child should be Married after Attaining Legal Age*	*Number*	*Percentage*
1.	Strongly Disagree	021	07.0
2.	Disagree	048	16.0
3.	Agree	199	66.3
4.	Strongly Agree	032	10.7
	Total	300	100

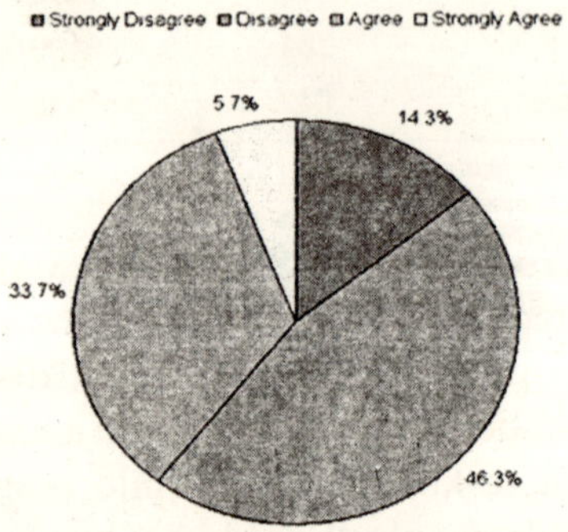

Figure 2. Opinion about Provision of Property for Girl Child

Table 30
Distribution of Respondents according to Their Opinion About Provision of Property for Girl Child

S.No.	*Girl Child must be Provided Property*	*Number*	*Percentage*
1.	Strongly Disagree	043	14.3
2.	Disagree	139	46.3
3.	Agree	101	33.7
4.	Strongly Agree	017	05.7
	Total	300	100

It is clear from Table 30 that, in all 182 or 60.6 per cent of the respondents express disagreement with the view that girl child must be given a share in the property. The number of those who express agreement i.e., 118 (39.4 per cent) only. In other words, the majority are against providing property to the girl child, give her share in property (Fig. 2).

Table 31
Distribution of Respondents according to Their Opinion about Giving Dowry for Girl Child's Marriage

S.No.	*Parents should not give Dowry for Girl Child's Marriage*	*Number*	*Percentage*
1.	Strongly Disagree	017	05.7
2.	Disagree	059	19.7
3.	Agree	187	62.3
4.	Strongly Agree	037	12.3
	Total	300	100

From the Table 31, it is clear that 224 respondents in all (62.3 + 12.3) agree that parents should not give dowry for the girl child's marriage. Those who disagree and are in favour of giving dowry are only 76 or 25.4 per cent. This is an encouraging and heartening development, and indicates some attitudinal change.

The Table 32 shows that 212 (25 + 187 or 8.3 + 62.3%) respondents do not agree that girls' views must be considered in the selection of life partners. Those who disagree are in the great majority. Only 88 respondents corresponding to 29.3 per cent of the total want the girls' views to be considered. Regarding dress, food and recreation, 188 respondents (30 + 158 corresponding to 62.7%) are not in favour of considering girls' views. The remaining 122 are in favour of the idea. Thus, the results clearly shows that more parents are not willing to consider the ideas of girl child regarding the selection of life partner, such small issues as dress, food, recreation. In general, in most of these issues, the views of boys are taken into consideration.

Table 32
Distribution of Respondents according to their Opinion Regarding Views of Girl Child in the Selection of Life Partner and Dress, Food and Recreation

S.No.	Respondents Opinion	Regarding Life Partner		Regarding Dress, Food, etc.	
		No.	Percentage	No.	Percentage
1.	Strongly Disagree	025	08.3	030	10.0
2.	Disagree	187	62.3	158	52.7
3.	Agree	085	28.3	095	31.7
4.	Strongly Agree	003	01.0	017	05.7
	Total	300	100	300	100

Table 33
Distribution of Respondents according to Their Opinion about Girl Child Having Friends of her Own Sex and of the Opposite Sex for Social Interaction

S.No.	Girl Child can have Friends	Girl Child can have Friends of Same Sex only		Girl Child can have Friends from Opposite Sex also	
		No.	Percentage	No.	Percentage
1.	Strongly Disagree	017	05.7	063	21.0
2.	Disagree	021	07.0	186	62.0
3.	Agree	168	56.0	036	12.0
4.	Strongly Agree	094	31.3	015	05.0
	Total	300	100	300	100

Table 33 gives details about the views of the respondents on a rather sensitive issue, namely the friends that a girl child can have for social interaction. The question whether she should have friends only of her sex or have friends of the opposite sex. In the sample of the study, as the table shows, 262 respondents (168 + 94 corresponding to 87.3 per cent) who contribute the vast majority, hold that girls can have friends of their sex only, while the remaining 38 respondents who form a very small minority disagree with this view. Regarding having friends among the opposite sex as many as 249 (63 +

186) respondents who form 83% of the sample, oppose strongly girls having friends among boys. The remaining 51 (36 + 15) respondents, again forming a small minority, agree that girls can have friends among boys. The opposition of so many parents who are also teachers to girls having friends among boys could be due to more than one cause : the hold that narrow traditional customs, cultural values and prevailing social conditions girl children may face threats from boys under the guise of friendship, and thus feel insecure and the feeling that they are safe and secure among friends of their own sex.

RESPONDENT'S OPINION ABOUT THEIR GIRL CHILD'S PSYCHOLOGICAL DEVELOPMENT

Table 34
Distribution of Respondents according to Their Opinion about Developing Good Personality of Girl Child

S.No.	*Importance of Respondents Opinion*	*Developing Personality is Important*		*Parents can Influence the Personality*	
		No.	*Percentage*	*No.*	*Percentage*
1.	Strongly Disagree	001	00.3	001	00.3
2.	Disagree	034	11.3	140	46.7
3.	Agree	207	69.3	131	43.7
4.	Strongly Agree	058	19.3	028	09.3
	Total	300	100	300	100

It is clear from the Table 34 that, the majority (69.3 per cent) of the respondents 'agree' that developing a good personality means good adjustment behaviour, helping or supporting nature having self-decision making capacity, being responsible, etc., which is very necessary to a girl child. This adaptability behaviour helps the girl child for better adjustment at critical situations and adjust with new persons at in-laws house after marriage, followed by 19.30 per cent of respondents who 'strongly agree'. Regarding parents' influence on personality development, 46.7 per cent of the respondents 'disagree'.

However, more than half of the respondents (53 per cent (43.7 + 9.3)) agree that parents can influence the development of personality of the girl child.

Table 35
Distribution of Respondents according to Their Opinion about Training Girl Child Crisis Management and Developing Self-esteem

S.No.	*Respondents' Opinion*	*Parents must Train Girl Child in Crisis Management*		*Parents must Develop Self-esteem in Girls*	
		No.	*Percentage*	*No.*	*Percentage*
1.	Strongly Disagree	005	01.7	006	02.0
2.	Disagree	124	41.3	116	38.7
3.	Agree	145	48.3	134	44.7
4.	Strongly Agree	026	08.7	044	14.7
	Total	300	100	300	100

Table 35 reveals that 145 respondents (48.3 per cent) 'agree' that parents must train the girl child in crisis management. But, 124 respondents (41.3 per cent) 'disagree' with that view. Regarding parents must develop self-esteem in the girl child, 134 respondents (44.7 per cent) 'agree' with the view but 116 respondents (38.7 per cent) 'disagree' with it. This table clearly shows that training in crisis management for girls is essential which is more appropriate in the present context also. Further, the respondents also are of the opinion that 'crisis management' is a self-acquired skill and enough scope should be provided to girl child by the parents to develop the necessary skills, which automatically develops one's self-confidence and self-esteem.

From Table 36, it is clear that, 149 or 49.7 per cent of the respondents 'agree' that parents must be friendly with the girl child but 105 or 35 per cent of them 'disagree' with it. Regarding the view that parents should not compel girls to do household work 124 or 41.3 per cent of the respondents 'agree' with it but 98 or 32.7 per cent 'disagree' with it. From the table, it may be learnt that 190 (149 + 41) or 63.4% (49.7 + 13.7 per cent) of the respondents intend to be friendly with their girl children which helps to develop good understanding between parents and children. Further, 161 (124 + 37)or 53.6 per cent (41.3% + 12.3%) of the respondents have the opinion that parents should not compel girls to do household work and that it is the responsibility of all the members of the family. But the remaining 139 (98 + 41) or 46.4% (32.7 + 13.7 per cent) disagree with the view, implying that household work is the responsibility of women only.

Table 36

Distribution of Respondents according to Their Opinion Regarding the View that Parents must be Friendly with Girl Children and should not Compel them to Do Household Work

S.No.	*Respondents Opinion*	*Parents must be Friendly*		*Parents should not Compel Girl Child to do Household Work*	
		No.	*Percentage*	*No.*	*Percentage*
1.	Strongly Disagree	005	01.7	041	13.7
2.	Disagree	105	35.0	098	32.7
3.	Agree	149	49.7	124	41.3
4.	Strongly Agree	041	13.7	037	12.3
	Total	300	100	300	100

Table 37

Distribution of Respondents according to their Opinion about Parents Punishing Girl Children when they do not Study and Misbehave

S.No.	*Respondents Opinion*	*Punish Girl Children for not Studying*		*Punish Girl Children for Misbehavious*	
		No.	*Percentage*	*No.*	*Percentage*
1.	Strongly Disagree	003	01.0	001	00.3
2.	Disagree	060	20.0	059	19.7
3.	Agree	188	62.7	183	61.0
4.	Strongly Agree	049	16.3	057	19.0
	Total	300	100	300	100

Table 37 clearly shows that, as many as 237 (188 + 49) respondents corresponding to 79 per cent 'agree' that parents must punish girls when they do not study. But only 63 or 21 per cent do not agree with it. Regarding punishment when girls misbehave, the majority of respondents (183 + 57 or 61% + 19%) are in favour of it. But only 60 (59 + 1) corresponding to 20 per cent 'disagree' with it. The results reveal that the majority of the respondents favour punishment when girl children do not study or when they misbehave. When asked what type of punishment they would suggest, most of them say that it ranges from scolding to beating depending on the situation.

Respondents' Opinion about Their Girl Child's Employment Support

Table 38
Distribution of Respondents according to Their Opinion about Providing Training for Girl Children in Job-oriented Courses Only

S.No.	*Girls should be Trained in Job-oriented Courses Only*	*Number*	*Percentage*
1.	Strongly Disagree	007	02.3
2.	Disagree	013	04.3
3.	Agree	169	56.3
4.	Strongly Agree	111	37.0
	Total	300	100

It is clear from Table 38 that, as many as 280 (169 who agree and 111 who strongly agree) corresponding to 93.3 per cent of the respondents 'agree' that girl child must be provided job-oriented training. Those who do not favour this opinion are in a negligible minority (7 + 13, 6.6 per cent). This overwhelming support to job-oriented training for girls may be because the respondents think that girls also need economic security for which job-oriented training is important. It also brings them a measure of economic independence.

From Table 39, it is clear that, 54.3 per cent 'disagree' with the idea of investing large amount in special job training courses for girl children, but 36.3 per cent 'agree' with the idea.

Regarding depositing money for jobs, a majority of respondents (65.3 per cent) 'disagree' with the idea while 29.7 per cent 'agree' with it. This shows that a majority of the parents are not willing to provide money security for their girl child to secure jobs.

Table 39
DIstribution of Respondents according to their Opinion about Investment in Special Job Training for Girl Child and Depositing Money for Jobs

S.No.	*Respondents' opinion*	*Investment in Special Job Training for Girl Child*		*Investment in Money Deposits for Girl Child*	
		No.	*Percentage*	*No.*	*Percentage*
1.	Strongly Disagree	015	05.0	008	02.7
2.	Disagree	163	54.3	196	65.3
3.	Agree	109	36.3	089	29.7
4.	Strongly Agree	013	04.3	007	02.3
	Total	300	100	300	100

Further, the results show that the respondents are willing to join their girl child in job-oriented courses, but they do not want to invest large amount in job training courses and provide money deposits for jobs. It may be because after marriage the girl child will be living with her husband or in-laws and the parents cannot expect any financial support from her (Fig. 3).

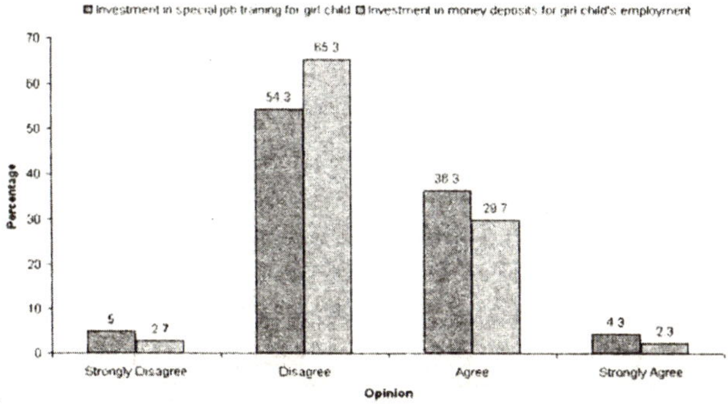

Figure 3. Opinion about Investment in Special Job Training for Girl Child and depositing Money for Jobs.

It is clear from Table 40 that, 66.3 per cent of the respondents 'agree' that the girl child must be provided training to get jobs like teaching, nursing etc., followed by 20.7 per cent who 'strongly agree' with this opinion. Regarding education to get jobs like collector, doctor, etc., 58 per cent 'agree' that the girl child must be provided education which enables them to become collectors, doctors, engineers, lecturers, etc., followed by 22 per cent 'strongly agree' with this opinion for that. So, the results clearly shows that most respondents feel that the girl child must be provided training or education in teaching, nurses, lecturers, doctors, etc. This clearly shows that the respondents prefer the above mentioned jobs as more suitable for girl children.

Table 40
Distribution of Respondents according to Their Opinion of Girl Child Training to Get Jobs Such as Teaching and Nursing or to Become High Officials Like Collector, etc.

S.No.	*Respondents' Opinion*	*Prefer Jobs in Teaching, Nursing, etc.*		*Prefer Jobs Such as Collector or Doctor, etc.*	
		No.	*Percentage*	*No.*	*Percentage*
1.	Strongly Disagree	005	01.7	016	05.3
2.	Disagree	034	11.3	044	14.7
3.	Agree	199	66.3	174	58.0
4.	Strongly Agree	062	20.7	066	22.0
	Total	300	100	300	100

It is clear from Table 41 that, 60.3 per cent of the respondents 'disagree' that girls should take up jobs like conductors, drivers, etc., but 34.3 per cent 'agree' with the opinion. Regarding taking up jobs like marketing executives or other marketing jobs, etc., 62 per cent of the respondents 'disagree' with that idea, but 31 per cent 'agree' with it. From the results, it is clear that more than three-fifth of the respondents do not favour their girls accepting jobs like conductor, driver, marketing executives, etc. It may be that these jobs are more physically stressful/risky and traditionally not acceptable to womenfolk, etc. (Fig. 4).

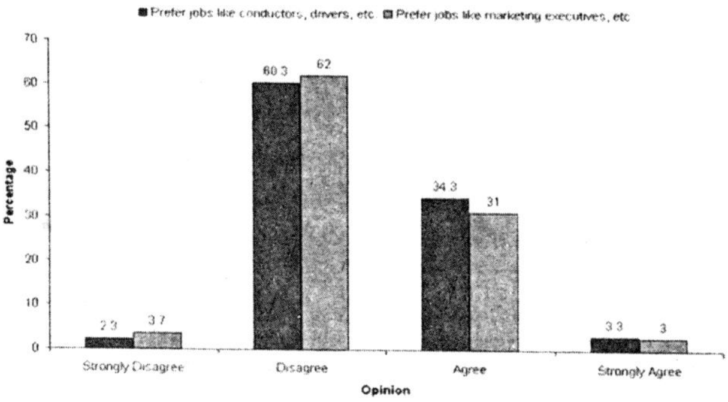

Figure 4. Opinion about Girls taking up of Jobs like Conductor, Driver or Marketing Jobs, etc.

Table 41
Distribution of Respondents according to Their Opinion about Girls Taking up of Jobs Like Conductor, Driver, Or Marketing Jobs, etc.

S.No.	*Respondents' Opinion*	*Prefer Jobs Like Conductors, Drivers, etc.*		*Prefer Jobs Like Marketing Executives, etc.*	
		No.	*Percentage*	*No.*	*Percentage*
1.	Strongly Disagree	007	02.3	011	03.7
2.	Disagree	181	60.3	186	62.0
3.	Agree	103	34.3	093	31.0
4.	Strongly Agree	009	03.0	010	03.3
	Total	300	100	300	100

Respondents' Opinion about Government Welfare Schemes for Girls

It is clear from Table 42 that a majority of the respondents i.e., 84.6 per cent (160 + 94) 'agree' that free education to girls upto the degree is very beneficial to them. The results clearly show that the respondents favour free education for girls upto the degree as it helps them to obtain higher education, and also increases the literacy rate of women.

Table 42
Distribution of Respondents according to Their Opinion that Free Education for Girls Upto Degree Level is Very Beneficial to Them

S.No.	Opinion about Free Education for Girl Child upto Degree	Number	Percentage
1.	Strongly Disagree	006	02.0
2.	Disagree	040	13.3
3.	Agree	160	53.3
4.	Strongly Agree	094	31.3
	Total	300	100

It is clear from Table 43 that, a little above half of the respondents (52.3 per cent) 'agree' that 'Balika Samrakshna Pathakam' is very useful to balance the sex ratio and reduce gender discrimination, but 33.3 per cent of them 'disagree' with it. The results clearly indicate that a majority of the respondents think that the 'Balika Samrakshna Pathakam' is useful, because this programme shares the burden of expenditure on the girl child's education, etc.

Table 43
Distribution of Respondents according to Their Opinion about Balika Samrakshana Pathakam

S.No.	Opinion about Balika Samrakshana Pathakam	Number	Percentage
1.	Strongly Disagree	014	04.7
2.	Disagree	100	33.3
3.	Agree	157	52.3
4.	Strongly Agree	029	09.7
	Total	300	100

Table 44 shows that, 48.7 per cent of the respondents 'disagree' with the view that 'Kishora Balika Scheme' encourages employment skills, opportunities and health awareness in girl children. But, 41 per cent of the respondents 'agree' and favour the scheme. Regarding the opinion that Kishora Balika Scheme increases awareness of family life education of girl children, 48.3 per cent of the respondents 'disagree' with that opinion. But, 38.7 per cent 'agree' with it. Though the parentage of those who 'disagree' is high, it is only marginally so, but these respondents, may be ignorant of the scheme.

Table 44
Distribution of Respondents according to their Opinion of Kishora Balika Scheme

S.No.	*Respondents' opinion*	*Kishore Balika Scheme Increases Employment Opportunities*		*Awareness of Family Life Education Due to Kishore Balika Scheme*	
		No.	*Percentage*	*No.*	*Percentage*
1.	Strongly Disagree	016	05.3	027	09.0
2.	Disagree	146	48.7	145	48.3
3.	Agree	123	41.0	116	38.7
4.	Strongly Agree	015	05.0	012	04.0
	Total	300	100	300	100

Table 45
Distribution of Respondents according to Their Opinion of Apni Beti Apna Desh Programme

S.No.	*Opinion of Apnabeti Apnadesh Programme*	*Number*	*Percentage*
1.	Strongly Disagree	026	08.7
2.	Disagree	145	48.3
3.	Agree	114	38.0
4.	Strongly Agree	015	05.0
	Total	300	100

It is observed from Table 45 that 48.3 per cent or 145 respondents 'disagree' that 'Apni Beti Apna Desh Programme' is very useful to rehabilitate the girls who have been rescued from child labour and brothel homes, but 38 per cent or 114 respondents on the contrary 'agree' that the programme does serve its purpose. From the results, it is clear that 171 respondents in all do 'not agree' that 'Apni Beti Apna Desh' programmes are beneficial, either because they are not aware about the programme or not satisfied with the implementation of the programme.

Table 44 shows that, 48.7 per cent of the respondents 'disagree' with the view that 'Kishora Balika Scheme' encourages employment skills, opportunities and health awareness in girl children. But, 41 per cent of the respondents 'agree' and favour the scheme. Regarding the opinion that Kishora Balika Scheme increases awareness of family life education of girl children, 48.3 per cent of the respondents 'disagree' with that opinion. But, 38.7 per cent 'agree' with it. Though the parentage of those who 'disagree' is high, it is only marginally so, but these respondents, may be ignorant of the scheme.

Table 46
Distribution of Respondents according to Their Opinion about Implementation of the Act on Pre-natal Diagnostic Test to Prevent Female Foeticide

S.No.	*Opinion about Implementation of the Act on Pre-natal Diagnostic Test*	*Number*	*Percentage*
1.	Strongly Disagree	024	08.0
2.	Disagree	085	28.3
3.	Agree	153	51.0
4.	Strongly Agree	038	12.7
	Total	300	100

Table 46 reveals that as many as 191 respondents in all (corresponding to 63.7%) 'agree' that strict implementation of the Pre-natal Diagnostic Technique (Regulation Prevention and misuse Act, 1994) helps in reducing female foeticide. But the remaining 109 respondents (corresponding to 36.3 per cent) 'disagree' with that. The results show that a majority of the respondents are satisfied with the implementation of the Act.

It is clear from Table 47 that, 177 (157 + 20) or 59 per cent (52.3 + 6.7) of the respondents 'agree' that the constitutional provisions and human rights for girl child do reduce gender discrimination. However, 123 (16 + 107) or 41 (5.3 + 35.7) per cent of the respondents 'disagree' with that view. The results reveal that a majority of the respondents agree that the constitutional provisions and human rights help to reduce the gender discrimination and thus safeguard for girls children's interests and secure for them benefits from the various provision/laws enacted for their welfare.

Table 47
Distribution of Respondents according to their Opinion about Constitutional Provisions and Human Rights for Girl Child Intended to Reduce Gender Discrimination

S.No.	*Opinion about Constitutional Provisions and Human Rights for Girls and Reduction of Discrimination*	*Number*	*Percentage*
1.	Strongly Disagree	016	05.3
2.	Disagree	107	35.7
3.	Agree	157	52.3
4.	Strongly Agree	020	06.7
	Total	300	100

Table 48
Distribution of Respondents according to Their Opinion about National Policy for Children and Legal Enactment to Facilitate the Development of Girl Child

S.No.	*Opinion about National Policy for Children*	*Number*	*Percentage*
1.	Strongly Disagree	024	08.0
2.	Disagree	099	33.0
3.	Agree	166	55.3
4.	Strongly Agree	011	03.7
	Total	300	100

From Table 48, it is clear that, a majority of the respondents (177 or 59 per cent) 'agree' that the National Policy for Children and legal enactments facilitate the development of the girl child. But, 123 (24 + 99) or 41 per cent (8 + 33) 'disagree' with that opinion. Their disagreement may be due to the fact that inspite of National Policy for Children being in favour since 1974, still the girl child is lagging behind in terms of education, employment, health, etc. But as the results reveal a majority of the respondents feel that utilization of National Policy for Children and legal enactments to facilitate development of girl child has been fairly satisfactory in the society.

Table 49
Distribution of Respondents according to Their Opinion about Sufficiency of Welfare Measures for Girl Child by the Government and Non-government Organizations

S.No.	*Opinion about Welfare Measures by Government and Non-governmental Organizations*	*Number*	*Percentage*
1.	Strongly Disagree	104	34.7
2.	Disagree	109	36.3
3.	Agree	074	24.7
4.	Strongly Agree	013	04.3
	Total	300	100

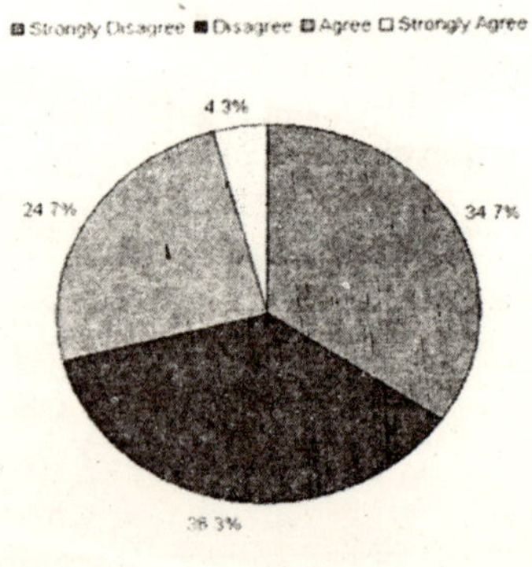

Figure 5. Opinion about Sufficiency of Welfare Measures for Girl Child by the Government and Non-Government Organisation

Table 49 reveals that a very considerable number of respondents (104 + 109) (34.7 + 36.3%) 'disagree' with the view that present welfare measures taken by government and non-governmental organizations are enough to improve the girl child's status. But 87 (74 + 13) or 29 per cent (247 + 43) of the respondents 'agree' that the government and non-government programmes are enough to improve the girl child's status. It is clear from the table that majority of the respondents feel that the present welfare programmes are not enough to improve the girl child's status nor do they give enough support to the girl child. More and specific intervention programmes are necessary to bring about changes in the attitudes of people to support and improve the girl child's status (Fig. 5).

Comparison of Mean Scores

Comparison of means of the 't' test was conducted to find out the significant differences between male and female respondents, joint and nuclear family respondents with regard to their opinion about the girl child's social participation, psychological development and government welfare schemes for girls.

Comparison of each factor among different educational groups, income groups, type of school the respondents are working etc., is made with the help One way of Analysis of Variance (ANOVA) with regard to the respondents opinion about the girl child's education, health and nutritional care, social participation, psychological development, employment support and government welfare schemes for girls.

Table 50

Variable	*Type of School*	*N*	*Mean*	*S.D.*	*Score*	*df*	*Mean Square*	*'F' Value*	*'P' Value*	*Result*
Respondents opinion about their girl child's education	Elementary School	150	37.1533	3.6060	Between groups	2	45.509	4.258	0.05	Significant at 5% level
	Upper Primary School	90	38.3444	2.7444	within groups	297	10.689			
	High School	60	38.8833	3.0989						

Regarding Hypothesis 1, ANOVA is computed to find out whether the respondents' opinion about the girl child's education differs by the type of school they are working in. The mean scores, standard deviation and statistical test results on opinion regarding the girl child's education are shown in Table 50.

Hypothesis: The respondents opinion about the girl child's education is significantly influenced by type of school they are working.

It is clear from Table 50 that, a high mean score for opinion about their girl child's education (38.8833) is found in the case of respondents who are working in high schools. The mean scores of opinion about the girl child's education differ significantly at 5 per cent level for different types of schools where respondents are working. So, the results prove the hypothesis that the respondents' opinion about the girl child's education is significant at 5 per cent level for different types of schools where respondents are working. So, the results prove the hypothesis that the respondents' opinion about the girl child's education is significantly influenced by type of school they are working in. It is observed that, the type of school, that is, high school provides more exposure to teachers (respondents) to understand the need of education for girl children than teachers who are working in lower level schools such as elementary schools and upper primary schools. Hence, we can conclude that 'the teachers who are working in high schools have better opinion about the girl child's education'.

Regarding Hypothesis 2, ANOVA is computed to find out whether the respondents' opinions about the girl child's education differ from one another by the type of training they have undergone. ANOVA Table 50 shows the mean, standard deviation, statistical test results of opinions about their girl child's education according to the type of training the respondents have undergone.

Hypothesis: The respondents' opinion about the girl child's education differs according to the training they have undergone.

Table 51 reveals that, a high mean score for opinion about the girl child's education (38.6154) is found in the case of respondents who have undergone M.Ed. training. The mean scores of opinion about girl child's education differ significantly at 5 per cent level among different types of training undergone. So, we accept the hypothesis and conclude that the respondents' opinions about the girl child's education differ according to the training they have undergone. There is a relationship between the type of training received by the respondents and their opinion about the girl child's education because higher training facilitates the respondents to develop a wider outlook on societal situations, which enables them to have better opinion regarding their girl child's education. So, 'the teachers who received higher educational training have a better opinion about girl child's education'.

Table 51

Variable	*Training received by the respondents*	*N*	*Mean*	*S.D.*	*Score*	*Df*	*Mean Square*	*'F' Value*	*'P' Value*	*Result*
Respondent's opinion about their girl child's educational status	Teacher training	50	36.3600	3.3671	Between groups	4	35.767	3.379	0.010	Significant at 5% level
	B.Ed.	183	38.0000	3.1501						
	M.Ed.	26	38.6154	3.0473						
	Technical Training	13	38.1538	3.8911	Within groups	295	10.584			
	BP.Bd. etc.	28	37.0357	3.5848						

Regarding Hypothesis 3, ANOVA is performed to find out whether the respondents' opinion about girl child's education differs with the number of daughters they have. The mean, standard deviation and statistical tests result of the opinion of the girl child's education according to the number of daughters the respondents have are shown in Table 51.

Hypothesis: The respondent's opinion about the girl child's education is significantly influenced by the number of daughters they have.

Table 52

Variable	*No. of Daughters*	*N*	*Mean*	*S.D.*	*Score*	*df*	*Mean Square*	*'F' Value*	*'P' Value*	*Result*
Respondents opinion about their girl child's education	1	179	37.9609	3.0765	Between groups	3	46.222	4.376	0.005	Significant at 1% level
	2	90	37.8111	3.2113						
	3	24	36.2500	4.2144						
	4 and above	7	34.4286	4.3916						
					Within groups	296	10.563			

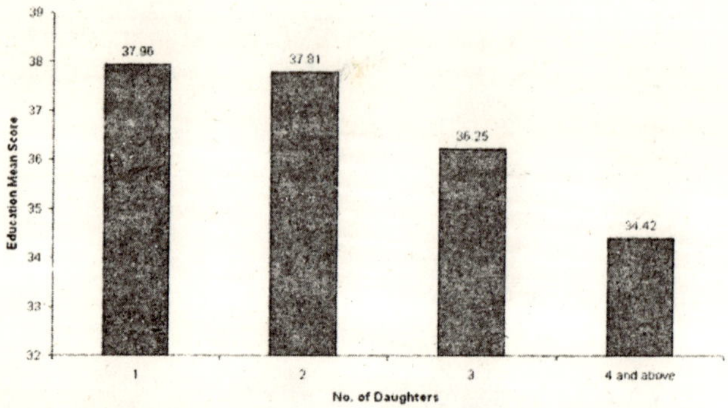

Figure 6. Mean Score Distribution according to Respondents Opinion about their Girl Child's Social Participation.

From Table 52, it is clear that a high mean score for respondent's opinion about the girl child education (37.9609) is found in the case of respondents who have only one daughter. The mean scores of the respondents opinions about the girl child's education according to the number of daughters they have differ significantly at 1 per cent level. So, we accept the hypothesis and conclude that the respondents' opinion about the girl child's education is significantly influenced by the number of daughters they have. The number of daughters influences the respondents' opinion about the daughters' education, because educating more girls is a difficult task because of the educational expenditure involved. So, that 'the respondents who have one daughter only have a better opinion regarding the girl child's education than those who have more daughters' (Fig. 6).

To test Hypothesis-4, the data on the respondents' opinions about the girl child's education is computed with ANOVA. The mean, standard deviation and statistical test results of the opinion about the girl child's educational status according to their income level are given in Table 52.

Hypothesis: The respondent's opinion about their girl child's education is dominantly influenced by their income level.

Table 53

Variable	*Income of the Respondent*	*N*	*Mean*	*S.D.*	*Score*	*df*	*Mean Square*	*'F' Value*	*'P' Value*	*Result*
Respondent's opinion on their girl child's education	Upto Rs.3000	49	38.9592	3.4337	Betwen groups	4	39.903	3.790	0.005	Signicant at 1% level
	Rs.3001-6000	61	36.9016	3.3000						
	Rs.6001-9000	92	37.5543	3.2152						
	Rs.9001-12000	67	38.1343	3.3070	Within Groups	295	10.528			
	Rs.12001-and above	31	36.7419	2.7321						

From Table 53 it is observed that a high mean score for the respondents' opinion about the girl child education (38.9592) is indicated in the case of 'upto Rs. 3,000' income group. The mean scores of income groups for opinion about the girl child's education differ significantly at 1 per cent level. So, we accept the hypothesis, and it follows that the respondent's opinion about the girl child's education is dominantly influenced by their income level. Education is an important component of the overall wellbeing of any person. Generally, low income persons tend to give a bright future for their children and education is the chief source of income so they encourage and support their girl children education as they have well experienced the hardships of low income. Thus, the low income respondents have a better supportive opinion about the girl child's education.

To test Hypothesis-5, ANOVA is performed to find out whether the respondent's opinion about the girl child's health and nutritional care differs with varying family income groups of respondents. The mean, standard deviation and statistical test result of the opinion of the respondent's regarding the girl child's health and nutritional care are given in Table 53.

Hypothesis: The respondent's opinion about the girl child's health and nutritional care is influenced by their family income.

Table 54

Variable	*Respondents Family Income*	*N*	*Mean*	*S.D.*	*Score*	*df*	*Mean Square*	*'F' Value*	*'P' Value*	*Result*
Respondent's opinion about their girls child's health and nutritional care	≤ Rs. 5,000	39	22.4103	1.6176						
	Rs. 5,001-10,000	105	22.1045	1.5685	Between groups	3	4.184			
	Rs. 10,001-15,000	81	22.6173	3.7033				0.675	0.568	Not Significant
	Rs. 15,001 & above	75	22.2267	2.2740	Within groups	296	6.200			

It is clear from Table 54 of ANOVA that, the mean score for the respondents' opinion about health and nutritional care is observed. In the case of respondents who have a family income of Rs. 10000 to Rs.15,000 per month, the mean score does not differ significantly among various family income groups of the respondents. So we reject the hypothesis and conclude that the respondent's opinion about the girl child's health and nutrition care is not influenced by the family income level. Thus, 'the respondents think that irrespective of one's family income one has to provide sufficient health and nutritional care for the girl child' which is essential for her growth and development.

Regarding Hypothesis-6, comparison of respondents' opinion about the girl child's health and nutritional care according to their family size has been carried out with the help of ANOVA. Table 54 shows the mean, standard deviation, statistical test results of the respondents opinion about the girl child's health and nutritional care in this regard.

Hypothesis: The respondent's opinion about the girl child's health and nutritional care is significantly influenced by the size of their family.

Table 55

Variable	*Family Size Respondent*	*N*	*Mean*	*S.D.*	*Score*	*df*	*Mean Square*	*'F' Value*	*'P' Value*	*Result*
Respondent's opinion about their girl child's health and nutritional care.	1–3	14	22.5000	1.6525						
	4–6	215	22.1953	1.7823	Between groups	3	19.421			
	7–9	52	22.1923	2.5286				3.213	0.023	Significant at 5% level
	9 and above	19	24.0000	6.4464	Within groups	296	6.045			

Table 55 indicates that a high mean score of the respondents opinion about the girl child's health and nutritional care is observed in the case of families which have 9 and above members. The mean scores of the respondents' opinion about the girl child's health and nutritional care significantly differ at 5% level. So, we accept the hypothesis and conclude that the respondents' opinion about the girl child's health and nutritional care is significantly influenced by the size of the family. As members of a large family, a teacher may feel the importance of health and nutritional care. And there is enough scope to take preventive and supportive measures regarding health and nutrition as more people are available at home. So, 'the respondents who are part of large families have a better opinion about the girl child's health and nutritional care than others'.

Regarding Hypothesis-7, 't' test is conducted to find out whether there is any difference between male and female respondents regarding their opinion about the girl child's social participation. The mean, standard deviation and statistical test results of the respondents' opinion in this regard are given below.

Hypothesis: The respondent's opinion about the girl child's social participation is significantly influenced by the sex of the respondents.

Table 56

Variable	*Sex of the Respondents*	*N*	*Mean*	*S.D.*	*Score*	*Df*	*Mean Square*	*'F' Value*	*'P' Value*	*Result*
Respondent's opinion about their girl child's social participation	Male	150	41.9533	3.9854	Between groups	1	39.603			
					Within groups	298	17.192	2.304	0.130	Not Significant
	Female	150	42.6800	4.3013						

Table 56 reveals that, a high mean score (42.68) of the respondents' opinion regarding the girl child's social participation is observed in the case of the women respondents. The mean scores of respondents' opinions regarding the girl child's social participation do not significantly differ between men and women respondents. So, we reject the hypothesis, and conclude that the respondents' opinion about their girl child's social participation is not significantly influenced by the sex of the respondents. It may be due to the fact that both male and female are working as teachers and know the importance of social participation for girls. Further, the women respondents have a better opinion than men respondents regarding the girl child's social participation.

Regarding Hypothesis-8, ANOVA is performed to find out whether the respondents' opinion regarding the girl child's social participation differs according to their religion. The mean, standard deviation and statistical test results of the respondent's opinions regarding it are given below:

Hypothesis: The respondents' opinion about the girl child's social participation is influenced by their religion.

From Table 57, it is clear that a high mean score 43.3333 of the respondents' opinion regarding the girl child's social participation is observed in the case of Muslim respondents, followed by the Hindus showing 42.5726 mean score indicating a narrow difference between them. The mean scores of respondents' opinion regarding the girl child's social participation differs among various religious group respondents at 1% level. So, we accept the hypothesis, and conclude that 'the respondents' opinion of their girl child's social participation is influenced by their religion. In general, the Muslim community imposes some restrictions on social exposure of women. But, in the sample of the present study reveal that the Muslim respondents have a better opinion of social participation for their girl children, which is a positive sign towards the development of the girl child.

Table 57

Variable	*Religion*	*N*	*Mean*	*S.D.*	*Score*	*df*	*Mean Square*	*'F' Value*	*'P' Value*	*Result*
Respondent's opinion about their girl child's social participation	Hindu	234	42.5726	3.7607	Between groups	3	73.419			
	Muslim	24	43.3333	4.1772				4.397	0.005	Significant 1% level
	Christian	33	40.5758	5.7881						
	Jain, etc.	9	39.3333	4.6637	Within groups	296	16.698			

To test Hypothesis-9, ANOVA is conducted to find out whether the respondents' opinion about the girl child's social participation varies according to their marital status. The mean, standard deviation and statistical test results of the respondents' opinions regarding it according to their marital status are given in ANOVA Table 57.

Hypothesis: The respondents' opinion about the girl child's social participation is significantly influenced by their marital status.

From the above Table 58, it is clear that a high mean score (42.7889) of the respondents' opinion about the girl child's social participation is observed in the case of widow/widower respondents. The mean scores of respondent's opinion about the girl child's social participation differ according to their marital status at 1% level. So, we accept the hypothesis and conclude that the respondents' opinion about their girl child's social participation is significantly influenced by their marital status. The fact of being a widow/widower may have enabled respondent to perceive the need of social participation for the girl child to maintain her daily household activities, so that, these respondents have a better opinion about the girl child's social participation.

Table 58

Variable	*Marital Status*	*N*	*Mean*	*S.D.*	*Score*	*df*	*Mean Square*	*'F' Value*	*'P' Value*	*Result*
Respondent's opinion about their girls child's social participation	Married	272	42.3860	3.9389	Between groups	3	89.557	5.4126	0.001	Significant at 1% level
	Divorced/Separated	8	41.5000	3.7796						
	Widowed	18	42.8889	4.5230						
	Unmarried	2	31.0000	15.5563	Within groups	296	16.535			

Regarding Hypothesis-10, 't' test is conducted to find out whether there is any difference between the respondents' opinion about the girl child's social participation according to their family type. The mean, standard deviation, and statistical test results of their opinion regarding it are given below in the Table 58.

Hypothesis: The respondents' opinion of the girl child's social participation is significantly influenced by the type of family of the respondents.

Table 59

Variable	*Family Type*	*N*	*Mean*	*S.D.*	*Score*	*df*	*Mean Square*	*'F' Value*	*'P' Value*	*Result*
Respondent's opinion about their girl child's social participation	Joint	88	41.6250	4.9487	Between groups	1	59.575	3.479	0.063	Significant at 1% level
	Nuclear	212	42.6038	3.7535	Within groups	298	17.125			

From Table 59, it is clear that the mean score of the respondent's opinion about the girl child's social participation according to their type of family does not differ significantly. So, we reject the hypothesis. It is found that the respondent's type of family does not influence their opinion about the girl child's social participation. Generally, the joint family imposes some restrictions on the mobility of the girl child rather than nuclear families. This study also shows that the nuclear family respondents have a better opinion regarding the girl child's social participation than the joint family respondents (Fig. 7).

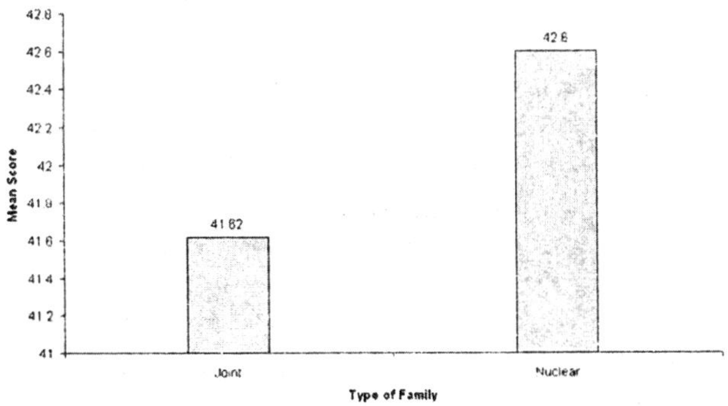

Figure 7. Mean Score Distribution according to Respondents Opinion about their Girl Child's Social Participation

To test Hypothesis-11, the mean scores and standard deviation are compared with the help of ANOVA. The mean, standard deviation and statistical test results of the respondents' opinion about the girl child's psychological development according to the respondents' educational level are shown in Table 59.

Hypothesis: The respondents' opinions of the girl child's psychological development varies according to their education.

Table 60

Variable	*Education*	*N*	*Mean*	*S.D.*	*Score*	*df*	*Mean Square*	*'F' Value*	*'P' Value*	*Result*
Respondent's opinion	Intermediate	49	22.3673	2.9347	Between groups	4	2.475			
about their	Graduate	169	22.3018	2.8636						
girl child's	P.G.	57	22.6491	4.3895	Within groups	295	11.401	0.217	0.929	Not Significant
Psychological	Ph.D.	7	22.8571	74.4929						
development	Pandit	18	22.833	3.0341						

From ANOVA Table 60, it is clear that the mean scores of the respondents regarding the girl child's psychological development does not differ significantly on the basis of their education. So, we reject the hypothesis, and conclude that, the respondents' opinion about the girl child's psychological development does not vary according to their education. It implies that, 'the respondents with different educational levels possess similar opinions about the girl child's psychological development'.

To test Hypothesis-12, 't' test is conducted to find out whether mean scores of the respondents' opinions about the girl child's psychological development differ between men and women respondents. The mean, standard deviation and statistical test results of their opinions regarding it are given in Table 60.

Hypothesis: The opinions about the girl child's psychological development differ between men and women respondents.

Table 61

Variable	*Sex of the Respondent*	*N*	*Mean*	*S.D.*	*Score*	*df*	*Mean Square*	*'F' Value*	*'P' Value*	*Result*
Respondent's opinion about their girl child's Psychological development	Male	150	22.4000	2.8918	Between groups	1	0.163			
	Female	150	22.4467	3.7783	Within the groups	298	11.319	0.014	0.904	Not Significant

It is clear from Table 61 that the mean scores of men and women respondents opinion about the girl child's psychological development are similar. So, we reject the hypothesis and conclude that 'the respondent's opinion of the girl child's psychological development does not differ between men and women respondents. It may be due to both male and female teachers being with similar background or exposure to traditional raring practices. They are in favour of socialization of the girl child regarding the girl child's psychological development'.

To test Hypothesis-13, ANOVA is conducted to find out whether the respondents' opinions about the girl child's employment support differ by the type of school they are working in. The mean, standard deviation and statistical test results of the respondents' opinions regarding it are given in ANOVA Table 61.

Hypothesis: The respondents' opinion about the girl child's employment support is dominantly influenced by the type of school they are working in.

From the above Table 62, it is clear that a high mean score (22.2444) is observed in the case of respondents who are working in upper primary schools. The mean scores of the respondents' opinion about their girl child's employment support differ significantly at 1% level. So, we accept the hypothesis and conclude that the respondents' opinion about the girl child's employment support is dominantly influenced by the type of school they are working in. It indicates that 'the respondents who are working in upper primary schools have a positive opinion about their girl child's employment support'.

Table 62

Variable	*Type of School*	*N*	*Mean*	*S.D.*	*Score*	*Df*	*Mean Square*	*'F' Value*	*'P' Value*	*Result*
Respondent's opinion about their girl child's employment support	Elementary School	150	20.5800	3.0964	Between groups	2	83.621			
	Upper primary School	90	22.2444	3.9670	Within groups	297	12.065	6.931	0.000	Significant at 1 % level
	High School	60	20.7167	3.5753						

To test Hypothesis-14, comparison of mean scores is carried out with the help of ANOVA to find out whether the respondents' opinions about the girl child's employment support differs according to their marital status. The mean, standard deviation and statistical test results of the respondent's opinion about the girl child's employment support are given in Table 62.

Hypothesis: The respondents' opinions about the girl child's employment support are influenced by their marital status.

It is observed from ANOVA Table 63 that a high mean score (21.1949) is noticed in the case of the respondents who are married and staying with their spouses. The mean score of the respondents' opinion about the girl child's employment support differ significantly at 5 per cent level according to their marital status. So, we accept the hypothesis that the respondents' opinion about the girl child's employment support is influenced by their marital status. It implies that, 'the respondents who are married and staying with their spouse have a better opinion of the girl child's employment support.

To test Hypothesis-15, an attempt has been made to examine the respondents' opinions about the government welfare schemes for girls among the gender groups with the help of 't' test. The mean, standard deviation and statistical tests results regarding the opinion of the respondent's about government welfare schemes for girl are given in the Table 63.

Table 63

Variable	Marital Status	N	Mean	S.D.	Score	Df	Mean Square	'F' Value	'P' Value	Result
Respondent's opinion about their girl child's employment support	Married	272	21.1949	3.5320	Between groups	3	42.545	3.476	0.016	Significant at 5% level
	Divorced/ Separated	8	20.0000	2.0702						
	Widowed	18	21.1111	2.9880	Within groups	296	12.240			
	Unmarried	2	13.5000	7.7782						

Hypothesis: There is a significant difference between men and women respondents' opinions about government welfare schemes for girls.

Table 64

Variable	Sex of the Respondent's	N	Mean	S.D.	Score	df	Mean Square	'F' Value	'P' Value	Result
Respondent's opinion about government welfare schemes for girls	Male	150	21.9400	5.0544	Between groups	1	220.163	10.200	0.002	Significant at 1% level
	Female	150	23.6533	4.1981	Within groups	298	21.585			

Table 64 reveals that a high mean score for opinion about government welfare schemes for girls (23.6533) is found in the case of women respondents. The mean scores of respondents' opinions of regarding them differ significantly at 1 per cent level. So, we accept the hypothesis, and conclude that, there is a significant difference between men an women respondents' opinions regarding the government welfare schemes for girls. As mothers and teachers, the women respondents have a better knowledge of government welfare schemes for the girl child, as in many cases the mother takes care of welfare measures of her children.

Regarding Hypothesis-16, ANOVA is performed to find out whether the respondents' opinions about the government welfare schemes for girls are influenced by their income. The mean, standard deviation and statistical test results of the respondents' opinion regarding them are given in Table 64.

Hypothesis: The respondents' opinions about the government welfare schemes are significantly influenced by their income.

Table 65

Variable	*Respondent's Income*	*N*	*Mean*	*S.D.*	*Score*	*df*	*Mean Square*	*'F' Value*	*'P' Value*	*Result*
Respondents opinion about government welfare schemes for girls	Upto Rs.3000	49	23.6735	5.1736	Between groups	4	82.550			
	Rs.3001-6000	61	23.3115	4.6959						
	Rs. 6001-9000	92	21.2283	5.2290	Within groups	295	21.432	5.530	0.001	Significant at 1% level
	Rs.9001-12000	67	23.5373	3.6445						
	Rs.12001 and above	31	23.4516	3.4141						

From ANOVA given in Table 65, it is clear that a high mean score of the respondent's opinion about the government welfare schemes for girls (23.6735) is found in the case of 'upto Rs. 3000 income group' of the respondents. The mean scores of income groups for their opinion about the government welfare schemes for the girl child differ significantly at 1 per cent level. So, we accept the hypothesis, and conclude that 'the respondents' opinions about the government welfare schemes are significantly influenced by their monthly income'. It implies that the respondents whose income does not so beyond Rs. 3000 are have been utilizing the Govt. welfare programmes for the girl child and that they have a good awareness of it.

Contribution of various Socio-economic Factors to Dependent Variables—A Regression Analysis

The main variables under the study viz., the respondents' opinions regarding the girl child's (1) education, (2) health and nutritional care, (3) social participation, (4) psychological development, (5) government welfare schemes for girls, are likely to be influenced by various personal factors (independent variables) like education, gender, income, religion, number of daughters, family size, marital status, type of school they are working in etc. In order to determine which of the above socio-economic factors (independent variables) have influence on the respondents' opinions about the girl child's education, health and nutritional care, social participation, psychological development, employment support, and about government welfare schemes for girls (dependent variables), step-wise regression analysis was carried out with the help of SPSS. A linear regression model has been fitted for each dimension linking if with the above factors. The contents of the regression tables are discussed below in this sub-section.

Results of Step-wise Regression

To know the contribution of certain socio-demographic variables to the respondent's opinion about the girl child's education, step-wise regression is carried out. A summary of the regression of different socio-demographic variables of the respondent's opinion about the girl child's education is presented in Table 66.

Table 66 indicates that the variables entered in the regression are number of daughters the respondents have, type of school they are working in and their family income. The regression coefficient of the number of daughters, the respondents have has a higher positive value (38.786) than the coefficient of type of school the respondent are working in and their family income. The R2 value is found to be 0.060 and the regression is found to be significant with F = 6.334 and P = 0.000. It means 'the number of daughters the respondents have has greater influence than the type of school they are working in and their family income in determining the respondents' opinion about the girl child's education. The coefficients are also significant as shown by the 't' values.

Table 66

Regression	*Regression Co-efficient*	*'t' value*	*Sig.*	*'R' Square value*	*'F' value*	*Sig. of 'F'*
Constant	38.786	52.770	.000			
Number of daughters	-0.725	-2.882	.004	0.060	6.334	0.000
Type of school	0.598	2.500	.013			
Family income	0.377	-2.005	.046			

Dependent Variables: Respondent's opinion of the girl child's education.

Variables Excluded from Regression: Age, Sex, Religion, Caste, Education, Family Type, etc.

Table 67

Regression	*Regression Co-efficient*	*'t' Value*	*Sig.*	*'R' Square Value*	*'F' Value*	*Sig. of 'F'*
Constant	21.34	40.773	0.000			
				0.013	3.944	0.048
Size of Family	0.443	1.986	0.48			

Dependent Variables: Respondents' opinions of the girl child's health and nutritional care.

Variables Excluded from Regression: Age, Sex, Education, Family Income, etc.

To assess the contribution of certain socio-economic factors to the respondent's opinion about the girl child's health and nutritional care, step-wise regression analysis is carried out. A summary of the regression of different personal variables of respondent's opinions about their girl child's health and nutritional care is shown in Table 67.

Table 67 shows that the most suitable predictor of the respondents' opinions about the girl child's health and nutritional care is the size of the family. With this predictor, R2 value is found to be 0.013, and the corresponding 'F' value is 3.944. The regression is significant with P = 0.048 for the 'F' value. The regression coefficient of size of the family is 0.443. It implies that 'the respondent's size of the family influences their opinions about the girl child's health and nutritional care. The coefficient is also significant as shown by the 't' values.

To find out the contribution of certain socio-economic factors to the respondents' opinions about the girl child's social participation, step-wise regression analysis is carried out. A summary of the regression of different socio-economic variables of the respondents' opinions about their girl child's social participation is given in Table 68.

Table 68

Regression	*Regression Co-efficient*	*'t' Value*	*Sig.*	*'R' Square Value*	*'F' Value*	*Sig. of 'F'*
Constant	44.609	66.335	0.000			
Religion	-0.883	-2.997	0.003	0.212	7.010	0.001
Number of daughters	-0.696	-2.193	0.029			

Dependent Variables: Respondent's opinion of the girl child's social participation.

Variables Excluded from Regression: Sex, Caste, Education, Family Type, Family Income, etc.

It is observed from Table 68 that, the variables entered in the regression are the respondents' religion, number of daughters they have. With these the predictors R2 value is found to be 0.212 and the corresponding 'F' value is 7.010. The regression is significant with 'P' value 0.001 for 'F' value.

The regression coefficient of their religion has a higher value 0.883 than the coefficient of number of daughters they have. It means 'the respondent's religion makes a higher contribution than the number of daughters they have in determining their opinion about their girl child's social participation. The coefficients are also significant as shown by their 't' values.

To asses the contribution of certain socio-economic factors to the respondents' opinion about the girl child's psychological development, step-wise regression analysis is carried out. A summary of the regression of different socio-economic variables to Psychological development is given in Table 69.

Table 69

Regression	*Regression Co-efficient*	*'t' Value*	*Sig.*	*'R' Square Value*	*'F' Value*	*Sig. of 'F'*
Constant	20.388	33.835	0.000			
Marital status	0.926	2.655	0.08	0.041	6.342	0.002
Purpose of loans taken	0.254	2.482	0.14			

Dependent Variables: Respondent's opinion of the girl child's psychological development.

Variables excluded from regression: Sex of the respondents, Religion, Education, Family Type, Family Income, etc.

Table 69 reveals that the variables entered in the regression are the respondent's marital status and the purpose of loans taken. With these two predictors R2 values is found to be 0.041 and the corresponding 'F' value is 6.342. The regression is significant with P = 0.002 for 'F' value. The regression coefficient of marital status has a higher value (0.926) than the coefficient of income. It implies that 'the respondents' marital status has a higher influence than the purpose of loan taken by the respondents in determining the opinion regarding their girl child's psychological development'. The coefficient are also significant as shown by the 't' values.

To assess the contribution of certain socio-economic factors to the respondent's opinion about government welfare schemes for girls, step-wise regression analysis carried out. A summary of the regression of different socio-economic variables to the respondents' opinion of government welfare schemes for girls is shown in the Table 70.

Table 70

Regression	*Regression Co-efficient*	*'t' Value*	*Sig.*	*'R' Square Value*	*'F' Value*	*Sig. of 'F'*
Constant	20.513	16.209	0.000			
Number of daughters	-0.940	-2.578	0.010			
				0.081	8.679	0.000
Type of School	0.971	2.888	0.004			
Sex of the respondents	1.381	2.556	0.011			

Dependent Variables: Respondents' opinions regarding government welfare programmes for girls.

Variables Excluded from Regression: Religion, Family Type, Family Income, Education, etc.

From Table 70, it may be found that, the variable selected for the regression arc the number of daughters, the type of school in which respondents are working and sex of the respondents. With these three predictors, R2 value is found to be 0.72 and the corresponding 'F' value is 8.679. The regression is significant with P = 0.000 for 'F' value. A comparison of the regression coefficients shows that 'the respondents' number of daughters rather than the type of school they are working in and sex of the respondents influence on their opinion regarding government welfare schemes for girls. The coefficients are also significant as shown in their 't' values.

5

Summary and Conclusions

Gender discrimination replicates itself from generation to generation, violates the rights of the girl child and chokes her further development. Persisting gender inequalities and existing cultural beliefs and practices permeate into almost every aspect of the growing girl's social, cultural environment and our value system.

The girl child is considered to be a lesser child in our society. She continues to be neglected at all levels and discrimination against her is rampant in all strata of society irrespective of class, caste and economic conditions. The existing profile of the girl child indicates declining female ratio, low nutritional status, high female mortality rate and school dropouts among girls.

The girl child is discriminated in India, as is evident form several social indicators. This is due to unfavourable attitudes prevailing in society, where the birth of a daughter is not celebrated in the same manner as the birth of a son. The sex ratio in the age group of 0-6 years indicates that for every 1000 boys there are only 927 girls. The situation is worse in the Northern and Western states. Enrollment of girls in schools is less than that of boys, and the dropout rate of girls is higher than that of boys, both at the primary and middle school levels.

According to Shukla and Ali (2006), "the future of any nation depends upon the sound development of children.

To build a civilized, cultural and happy society, we have to educate and train our children properly because tomorrow they would take the nation towards prosperity. Elimination of girl child discrimination and welfare of girl child at par with boy child have emerged as an important area of concern in today's civilized society. Hence, the Government and non-governmental organizations have been making efforts to provide legal and welfare measures to support girl child's development. The Child Marriage Restraint Act, 1929; the Dowry Prohibition Act, 1961; National Policy of Education, 1986; National Plan of Action for girl child for survival and protection development, 1991; the Prenatal diagnostic techniques (Prevention of Misuses) Act, 1994; Integrated Child Development Scheme, 1975; Cradle Baby Scheme, 1992; Balika Samridhi Yojana, 1997; Kasturba Gandhi Yojana, 1997; Kishori Shakti Yojana, 2000; Sarva Siksha Abhiyan, 2002 etc., are some of the steps initiated so far. Inspite of these and other measures, the situation of the girl child remains vulnerable.

To improve the status of the girl child, strict implementation of law is not enough as it will not change the mindset, especially of the propertied classes who want sons to 'carryon the family'. Gender sensitization through multiple campaigns and awareness programmes should be organized to promote the importance of girl child to encourage parents to educate their daughters and make them avail themselves of all facilities along with their counterparts. It is also necessary to promote gender sensitization by reducing negative attitudes towards the girl child from her school-going age, as it is crucial and most impressionable age when their attitudes and opinions are formed. In this regard, the teachers play an important role in creating awareness of gender equality among the students from childhood. Hence, considering the problem in its totality, an effort has been made in the present study entitled "Parents Opinion towards Girl Child – A Study amongst School Teachers in Tirupati" to know the opinion of teachers who are also parents of the girl child. It has aimed at knowing the respondents' socio-economic and demographic information and their opinion regarding their girl child's education, health and nutritional care, social participation, psychological development, employment support and opinion about welfare schemes for girls.

The study is descriptive and explorative in nature. With the help of stratified random sample by proportionate allocation, a sample of 300 teachers who have both a boy and girl child, and who are working in the schools of Tirupati were selected purposively for the present study. An interview schedule after pre-testing was used to collect the data from the respondents. Statistical analysis was carried out with the SPSS 9.0. Comparisons were made with 't' test and ANOVA, step-wise regression analysis was adopted in appropriate contexts. The major findings are presented hereunder:

MAJOR FINDINGS

1. A majority (78 per cent) of the respondents are Hindus (Table 1 of Chapter 4).
2. The vast majority (90.7 per cent) of the respondents are married and the spouses live together (Table 1 of Chapter 4).
3. A good majority (71 per cent) of the respondents live in nuclear families (Table 2 of Chapter 4).
4. A majority of the respondent families (72 per cent) consist of 4 to 6 members (Table 2 of Chapter 4).
5. A majority i.e., 81.3 per cent of the respondents have one son (Table 2 of Chapter 4).
6. A majority 61.3 per cent of the respondents have undergone B.Ed. training (Table 3 of Chapter 4).
7. A majority (82 per cent) of the respondents have some savings (Table 4 of Chapter 4).
8. A majority (62.3 per cent) of the respondents 'agree' that education is important for girls (Table 5 of Chapter 4).
9. More than half of the respondents (58.3 per cent) 'agree' that parents can reduce girls dropping out of school (Table 6 of Chapter 4).
10. A little less than three-fifths (57.3 per cent) of the respondents 'agree' with the statement that education

upto intermediate and graduation is not enough for girls (Table 7 of Chapter 4).

11. A majority (66.3 per cent) of the respondents 'agree' that parents must help in the education of girls (Table 13 of Chapter 4).
12. A little more than half (57 per cent) of the respondents 'agree' that reservations, free education and such programmes help girls to acquire education (Table 15 of Chapter 4).
13. The vast majority (99.4 per cent) of the respondents 'agree' that parents play an important role in girls' health (Table 17 of Chapter 4).
14. A majority i.e., 61.3 per cent of the respondents 'disagree' that regular health checkups are necessary for girls (Table 18 of Chapter 4).
15. A majority of the respondents (69.7 per cent) 'agree' that early treatment of health problems of their girl child is essential (Table 19 of Chapter 4).
16. A little less than half of the respondents (48.3 per cent) are 'disagree' with the view that home remedies are not enough for treatment (Table 20 of Chapter 4).
17. As many as 88.3 per cent of the respondents 'agree' that hospital treatment must be provided to girls (Table 21 of Chapter 4).
18. Almost nine-tenths (89 per cent) of the respondents favour nutritious diet for girls (Table 22 of Chapter 4).
19. A little above half of the respondents (56.7 per cent) 'agree' that additional diet like fruits, salads, etc. (Table 23 of Chapter 4) must be given to girl children.
20. A little above half of the respondents (53 per cent) are not in favour of giving pocket money to girls to purchase eatables along with other expenditure (Table 24 of Chapter 4).
21. A little above half of the respondents (57 per cent) of the respondents 'agree' that girls must participate in outdoor sports (Table 24 of Chapter 4).
22. A little above half (55.3 per cent) of the respondents 'agree' that girl child must participate in indoor games (Table 24 of Chapter 4).

23. A majority (63 per cent) of the respondents 'disagree' that the girl child needs training in dance and music (Table 25 of Chapter 4).
24. More than three fourths of the respondents (77 per cent) 'agree' that girls should be married only after their attaining legal age (Table 26 of Chapter 4).
25. A majority (60.6 per cent) of the respondents express disagreement with the view that the girl child must be given a share in the property (Table 27 of Chapter 4).
26. Nearly three-fourths (74.3 per cent) of the respondents 'agree' that parents should not give dowry for the girl child's marriage (Table 28 of Chapter 4).
27. A majority (70.6 per cent) of the respondents do not agree that girls' views must be considered in the selection of life-partners (Table 29 of Chapter 4).
28. A majority (87.3 per cent) of the respondents hold that girls can have friends of their sex only (Table 30 of Chapter 4).
29. A majority (69.3 per cent) of the respondents 'agree' that developing a sound and balanced personality which means good adjustment, self-decision making capacity, etc., is very necessary for the girl child (Table 34 of Chapter 4).
30. Very nearly eight-fifths (79 per cent) of the respondents 'agree' that parents must punish girls when they do not study (Table 37 of Chapter 4).
31. A huge majority of the respondents (80 per cent) are in favour of punishment when girls misbehave (Table 37 of Chapter 4).
32. A vast majority i.e., 93.3 per cent of the respondents 'agree' that the girl child must be provided job-oriented training (Table 38 of Chapter 4).
33. A majority (65.3 per cent) of the respondents 'disagree' with the idea of depositing money for jobs for their girl child (Table 39 of Chapter 4).
34. A majority of the respondents (66.3 per cent) 'agree' that the girl child must be provided training to get jobs like teaching, nursing, etc. (Table 40 of Chapter 4).

35. A majority (62 per cent) of the respondents 'disagree' with the idea of their daughters taking up jobs like marketing executives or other marketing jobs (Table 41 of Chapter 4).
36. More than three-fifths (63.7 per cent) of the respondents 'agree' that strict implementation of the Prenatal Diagnostic Technique (Regulation Prevention and Misuse Act, 1994) helps in reducing female foetic (Table 46 of Chapter 4).
37. A majority i.e., 71 per cent of the respondents 'disagree' with the view that, the welfare measures taken by the government and non-governmental organizations at present are enough to improve the girl child's status (Table 49 of Chapter 4).
38. The respondents who received higher educational training have a better opinion about girl child's education (Table 51 of Chapter 4).
39. The respondents who have one daughter only have a better opinion regarding the girl child's education than those who have more daughters (Table 52 of Chapter 4).
40. The women respondents have better opinion than men respondents regarding their girl child's social participation (Table 56 of Chapter 4).
41. The nuclear family respondents have better opinion regarding their girl child's social participation than the joint family respondents (Table 59 of Chapter 4).
42. The respondents with different educational levels possess similar opinions about the girl child's psychological development (Table 60 of Chapter 4).
43. The respondents who are working in upper primary schools have a positive opinion about their girl child's employment support (Table 61 of Chapter 4).
44. The women respondents have a better opinion of the government welfare schemes for girls (Table 64 of Chapter 4).
45. The number of daughters, the respondents have has greater influence than the type of school they are working and their family income in determining their

opinion about their girl child's education (Table 66 of Chapter 4).

46. The respondents' size of the family influences their opinion about their girl child's health and nutritional care (Table 67 of Chapter 4).

FINDINGS OF THE STUDY

Socio-Economic and Demographic Information

1. An equal number of respondents i.e., 50 per cent each are men and women (Table 1 of Chapter 4).
2. A majority (78 per cent) of the respondents are Hindus (Table 1 of Chapter 4).
3. A little more than half of the respondents (53.7 per cent) belong to the forward caste category (Kamma and Reddy) (Table 1 of Chapter 4).
4. The vast majority (90.7 per cent) of the respondents are married and the spouses live together (Table 1 of Chapter 4).
5. A good majority (71 per cent) of the respondents live in nuclear families (Table 2 of Chapter 4).
6. A majority of the respondent families (72 per cent) consist of 4 to 6 members (Table 2 of Chapter 4).
7. A mentionable number (59.7 per cent) of the respondents have one daughter (Table 2 of Chapter 4).
8. A majority i.e., 81.3 per cent of the respondents have one son (Table 2 of Chapter 4).
9. A recognizable number i.e., 59 per cent of the respondents are working in government-aided schools (Table 2 of Chapter 4).
10. A notable number i.e., 50 per cent of the respondents are working in elementary schools (Table 2 of Chapter 4).
11. More than half of the respondents (56.3 per cent) are graduates (Table 3 of Chapter 4).
12. A majority 61.3 per cent of the respondents have undergone B.Ed. training (Table 3 of Chapter 4).

13. A little more than one-fourth of the respondents i.e., 30.7 per cent belong to the income group of Rs. 6,001 to 9,000 per month (Table 3 of Chapter 4).
14. A little more than one-fourth of the respondents (35 per cent) have a monthly family income between Rs. 5,001 to 10,000 (Table 3 of Chapter 4).
15. A little less than two-fifths (38 per cent) do not have any other source of income than their monthly salary (Table 3 of Chapter 4).
16. A majority (82 per cent) of the respondents have some savings (Table 4 of Chapter 4).
17. A little more than half of the respondents (54.3 per cent) feel that their economic sources are partly adequate (Table 4 of Chapter 4).
18. A little more than one-fourth (29.3 per cent) of the respondents manage financial emergencies by raising loans from banks or from their own office (Table 4 of Chapter 4).
19. A little less than one-fifth of respondents (18 per cent) have raised loans for their sons' education, employment and business (Table 4 of Chapter 4).
20. A little more than one-fourth of the respondents (26.7 per cent) are repaying the loans in monthly installments (Table 4 of Chapter 4).

Respondents' Opinion About Their Girl Child's Education

1. A majority (62.3 per cent) of the respondents 'agree' that education is important for girls (Table 5 of Chapter 4).
2. More than half of the respondents (58.3 per cent) 'agree' that parents can reduce girls dropping out of school (Table 6 of Chapter 4).
3. A little less than three-fifths (57.3 per cent) of the respondents 'agree' with the statement that education upto intermediate and graduation is not enough for girls (Table 7 of Chapter 4).
4. Nearly half of the respondents (49.7) 'agree' that professional education is necessary for girls (Table 8 of Chapter 4).

5. A little more than two-fifths of the respondents (43.7 per cent) 'disagree' with the view that government school education is not enough for girl children (Table 9 of Chapter 4).
6. More than half of the respondents (57.3 per cent) express their willingness (Agree) to pay huge sums of money as donations for professional courses for girls (Table 10 of Chapter 4).
7. A little more than two-fifths (41.7 per cent) of the respondents are unwilling (disagree) to pay donations to professional courses for their girls outside the state (Table 11 of Chapter 4).
8. A little less than half of the respondents (48.7 per cent) favour the view that private school education is necessary for girls (Table 12 of Chapter 4).
9. A majority (66.3 per cent) of the respondents 'agree' that parents must help in the education of girls (Table 13 of Chapter 4).
10. A little more than half of the respondents (52 per cent) 'disagree' on private tuitions to be arranged for girls (Table 14 of Chapter 4).
11. A little more than half (57 per cent) of the respondents 'agree' that reservations, free education and such programmes help girls to acquire education (Table 15 of Chapter 4).
12. A little less than half (45.3 per cent) of the respondents 'disagree' with the view that study tours are essential for girls for their recreation and acquisition of knowledge (Table 16 of Chapter 4).
13. The respondents who are working in high schools have better opinion about the girl child's education (Table 50 of Chapter 4).
14. The respondents who received higher educational training have a better opinion about girl child's education (Table 51 of Chapter 4).
15. The respondents who have one daughter only have a better opinion regarding the girl child's education than those who have more daughters (Table 52 of Chapter 4).

16. The low income respondents (i.e., upto Rs. 3,000 per month) have better supportive opinion about the girl child's education (Table 53 of Chapter 4).
17. The number of daughters, the respondents have has greater influence than the type of school they are working and their family income in determining their opinion about their girl child's education (Table 66 of Chapter 4).

Respondents' Opinion About their Girl Child's Health and Nutritional Care

1. The vast majority (99.4 per cent) of the respondents 'agree' that parents play an important role in girls' health (Table 17 of Chapter 4).
2. A majority i.e., 61.3 per cent of the respondents 'disagree' that regular health checkups are necessary for girls (Table 18 of Chapter 4).
3. A majority of the respondents (69.7 per cent) 'agree' that early treatment of health problems of the girl child is essential (Table 19 of Chapter 4).
4. As many as 88.3 per cent of the respondents 'agree' that hospital treatment must be provided to girls (Table 21 of Chapter 4).
5. Almost nine-tenths (89 per cent) of the respondents favour nutritious diet for girls (Table 22 of Chapter 4).
6. A little above half of the respondents (56.7 per cent) 'agree' that additional diet like fruits, salads, etc. (Table 22 of Chapter 4) must be given to girl children.
7. A little above half of the respondents (53 per cent) are not in favour of giving pocket money to girls to purchase eatables along with other expenditure (Table 23 of Chapter 4).
8. The respondents think that irrespective of one's family income one has to provide sufficient health and nutritional care for the girl child (Table 54 of Chapter 4).
9. The respondents who are part of large families have a better opinion about their girl child's health and nutritional care than others (Table 55 of Chapter 4).

10. The respondents' size of the family influences their opinion about their girl child's health and nutritional care (Table 67 of Chapter 4).

Respondents Opinion about Their Girl Child's Social Participation

1. A little above half of the respondents (57 per cent) of the respondents 'agree' that girls must participate in outdoor sports (Table 24 of Chapter 4).
2. A little above half (55.3 per cent) of the respondents 'agree' that girl child must participate in indoor games (Table 24 of Chapter 4).
3. A majority (63 per cent) of the respondents 'disagree' that the girl child needs training in dance and music (Table 25 of Chapter 4).
4. Two-fifths of the respondents (40 per cent) 'disagree' with the idea that girl child needs training in martial arts (Table 25 of Chapter 4).
5. A little less than two fifths (37.7 per cent) of the respondents 'agree' that girl children must participate in competitions in local places (Table 26 of Chapter 4).
6. A little more than two-fifths (45.3 per cent) of the respondent's 'agree' that girls must participate in competitions in outstation places (Table 26 of Chapter 4).
7. A majority of the respondents (60 per cent) 'disagree' that there is no need for separate schools for girls (Table 27 of Chapter 4).
8. A majority (61.3 per cent) of the respondents 'agree' that training should be provided to the girl child in house-keeping (Table 28 of Chapter 4).
9. A majority (62.3 per cent) of the respondents 'agree' that the girl child needs training in marketing, payment of various bills and shopping (Table 28 of Chapter 4).
10. More than three fourths of the respondents (77 per cent) 'agree' that girls should be married only after their attaining legal age (Table 29 of Chapter 4).

11. A majority (60.6 per cent) of the respondents express disagreement with the view that the girl child must be given a share in the property (Table 30 of Chapter 4).
12. Nearly three-fourths (74.3 per cent) of the respondents 'agree' that parents should not give dowry for the girl child's marriage (Table 31 of Chapter 4).
13. A majority (70.6 per cent) of the respondents do not agree that girls' views must be considered in the selection of life-partners (Table 32 of Chapter 4).
14. A majority (62.7 per cent) of the respondents are not in favour of considering girls' views (Table 33 of Chapter 4).
15. A majority (87.3 per cent) of the respondents hold that girls can have friends of their sex only (Table 33 of Chapter 4).
16. As many as 83 per cent of the respondents oppose strongly girls having friends among boys (Table 33 of Chapter 4).
17. The respondents who are part of large families have a better opinion about their girl child's health and nutritional care than others (Table 55 of Chapter 4).
18. The women respondents have better opinion than men respondents regarding their girl child's social participation (Table 56 of Chapter 4).
19. The results of the study reveal that Muslim respondents have better opinion of social participation for their girl children (Table 57 of Chapter 4).
20. The respondents who are widows/widowers have better opinion about their girl child's social participation (Table 58 of Chapter 4).
21. The nuclear family respondents have better opinion regarding their girl child's social participation than the joint family respondents (Table 59 of Chapter 4).
22. The respondents' religion makes a higher contribution than their number of daughters they have to determining their opinion about their girl child's social participation (Table 68 of Chapter 4).

Respondents' Opinion About Their Girl Child's Psychological Development

1. A majority (69.3 per cent) of the respondents 'agree' that developing a sound and balanced personality which means good adjustment, self-decision making capacity, etc., is very necessary for the girl child (Table 34 of Chapter 4).
2. A little less than half (46.7 per cent) of the respondents 'disagree' that parents influence on the personality development of girls (Table 34 of Chapter 4).
3. A little less than half (48.3 per cent) of the respondents 'agree' that parents must train the girl child in crisis management (Table 35 of Chapter 4).
4. A little less than half (44.7 per cent) of the respondents 'agree' with the view that, parents must develop self-esteem in girls (Table 35 of Chapter 4).
5. A little less than half (49.7 per cent) of the respondents 'agree' that parents must be friendly with the girl children (Table 36 of Chapter 4).
6. A little above half (53.6 per cent) of the respondents have the opinion that parents should not compel girls to do household work (Table 36 of Chapter 4).
7. Very nearly eight-fifths (79 per cent) of the respondents 'agree' that parents must punish girls when they do not study (Table 37 of Chapter 4).
8. A huge majority of the respondents (80 per cent) are in favour of punishment when girls misbehave (Table 37 of Chapter 4).
9. The respondents with different educational levels possess similar opinions about the girl child's psychological development (Table 60 of Chapter 4).
10. The men and women respondents have similar opinion about their girl child's psychological development (Table 61 of Chapter 4).
11. The respondents' marital status has a higher influence than the purpose of loan taken by the respondents in determining their opinion regarding their girl child's psychological development (Table 69 of Chapter 4).

Respondent's Opinion About Their Girl Child's Employment Support

1. A vast majority i.e., 93.3 per cent of the respondents 'agree' that the girl child must be provided job-oriented training (Table 38 of Chapter 4).
2. A little above half (54.3 per cent) of the respondents 'disagree' with the idea of investing large amount in special job-training courses for girl children (Table 39 of Chapter 4).
3. A majority (65.3 per cent) of the respondents 'disagree' with the idea of depositing money for jobs for their girl child (Table 39 of Chapter 4).
4. A majority of the respondents (66.3 per cent) 'agree' that the girl child must be provided training to get jobs like teaching, nursing, etc. (Table 40 of Chapter 4).
5. A majority of the respondents (60.3 per cent) 'disagree' that girls should take up jobs like conductors, drivers, etc. (Table 41 of Chapter 4).
6. A majority (62 per cent) of the respondents 'disagree' with the idea of their daughters taking up jobs like marketing executives or other marketing jobs (Table 41 of Chapter 4).
7. The respondents who are working in upper primary schools have a positive opinion about their girl child's employment support (Table 62 of Chapter 4).
8. The respondents who are married and staying with tier spouses have better opinion about their girl child's employment support (Table 63 of Chapter 4).

Respondents Opinion About Government Welfare Schemes for Girls

1. A majority of the respondents i.e., 84.6 per cent 'agree' that free education to girls upto degree is very beneficial (Table 42 of Chapter 4).
2. A little above half of the respondents (52.3 per cent) 'agree' that 'Balika Samrakshna Pathakam' is very useful to balance the sex ratio and reduce gender discrimination (Table 43 of Chapter 4).

3. A little less than half of the respondents (48.7 per cent) of the respondents 'disagree' with the view that 'Kishora Balik Scheme encourages employment skills, opportunities and health awareness in girl children (Table 44 of Chapter 4).
4. A little less than half (48.3 per cent) of the respondents 'disagree' with the opinion that, Kishora Balik Scheme increases awareness of family life education of girl children (Table 44 of Chapter 4).
5. A little less than half (48.3 per cent) of the respondents 'disagree' Apni Beti Apna Desh programme is very useful to rehabilitate the girls who have been rescued from child labour and brothel homes (Table 45 of Chapter 4).
6. More than three-fifths (63.7 per cent) of the respondents 'agree' that strict implementation of the Prenatal Diagnostic Technique (Regulation Prevention and Misuse Act, 1994) helps in reducing female foetic (Table 46 of Chapter 4).
7. A majority of the respondents (59 per cent) 'agree' that the constitutional provisions and human rights for the girl child do reduce gender discrimination.
8. Almost three-fifths (59 per cent) of the respondents 'agree' that the national policy for children and legal enactment facilitate the development of the girl child (Table 48 of Chapter 4).
9. A majority i.e., 71 per cent of the respondents 'disagree' with the view that, the welfare measures taken by the government and non-governmental organizations at present are enough to improve the girl child's status (Table 49 of Chapter 4).
10. The women respondents have a better opinion of the government welfare schemes for girls (Table 64 of Chapter 4).
11. The respondents whose income does not 80 beyond Rs.3,000 per month have a better opinion about government welfare schemes for girls (Table 65 of Chapter 4).
12. The respondents' number of daughters rather than the type of school they are working in and the sex of the

respondents, influence their opinion regarding government welfare schemes for girls (Table 70 of Chapter 4).

CONCLUSION

The results of the present study indicate that a majority of the respondents are Hindus and are currently staying with their spouses in nuclear families. Most of the families (nearly three-fourths) consist of 4 to 6 members and above four-fifth respondents have one son. Nearly three-fifths are graduates and have undergone B.Ed. training and a little above four-fifths have some savings from their income. Education is crucial for the development of human resources. The results regarding the respondent's opinion about their girl child's education show that above three-fifths of the respondents believe that education is important for girls and an identical number of respondents feel that intermediate and graduation are the minimum education for the girl child and an equal number are agreed to pay donations for professional courses for the girl child. Around three-fifths of the respondents have the opinion that reservations, free education, etc., programmes helpful for girl child to acquire education. Further, the results of the present study show that the respondents who are working in high schools and have undergone higher training in education have a better opinion of their girl child's education.

Health and nutritional care is an essential component of facilitate good physical and psychological development of girl children. The results of the study reveal that 7 out of 10 of the respondents provide early treatment at hospitals to their girl children during illness. Further, the result shows that the respondent's size of the family influences the respondent's opinion about their girl child's health and nutritional care.

Regarding the respondents' views on there is no need of separate school for girls, three-fifths of the respondents 'disagree' with it. The study shows that three-fifths of the respondents 'disagree' with there is no need of separate schools for girl child means they emphasized the need of separate school for the girl child. Further, above three-fifths of the respondents state that the girl child must be provided training in both house keeping and marketing, payment of various bills and shopping, and similar chores etc. And above three-fifths of the respondents express the view that the girl child should be married after attaining legal age only. Further three-fifths of the respondents are against to giving dowry at the time of the marriage of the girl child and they are against giving an opportunity to their girl child to select her life-partner and to have friends of the opposite sex. The study also reveals that the women respondents have a better opinion regarding their girl child's social participation than their men counterparts.

The present study reveal that nearly seven out of ten of the respondents accept that development of personality of the girl child is essential and it has to be attended to. A little above three-fifths of the respondents favour punishment to their girl children when they do not study, and four-fifths of them opinioned that parents must punish their girl children when they misbehave. The results also reveal that the men and women respondents and those with different educational levels have similar opinion about their girl child psychological development.

The present study shows that above three-fifths of the respondents are not willing for providing money as deposit to get jobs for their girl child and they also state that the girl child must be provided training in teaching, nursing, etc. Three-fifths of the respondents do not prefer jobs like those of conductors, drivers, marketing executives etc., for their daughters as they are stressful and risky jobs. Further, respondents who are working in upper primary schools have a positive opinion about their girl child's employment support.

Regarding government welfare schemes, the findings of the present study revealed that above half of the respondents are with the opinion that 'free education upto degree for girl's is very beneficial for the girl child and as many also feel that the 'Balika Samrakshana Pathakam' is very useful to balance the sex ratio and to reduce gender discrimination. Further, the study discloses that the respondents who have low income (i.e., upto Rs. 3,000 per month) have a better opinion regarding government welfare schemes for girls.

SUGGESTIONS

It remains now to put forward certain suggestions to improve the lot of the girl child in our society. The suggestions are workable and are presented here as worth trying out.

The results of the present study of "Teachers' (Parent) opinion regarding their girl child's education" reveal that the respondents who have one daughter have a better opinion regarding it than those who have more daughters. Further, the respondents feel that minimum education upto intermediate and graduation are not enough for the girl child, and that reservations, free education etc., would also help them. Therefore, 'the government should provide enough scope for girls to pursue higher education like Post-graduation, technical education, etc., in a decentralized system. Because now-a-days to pursue higher education girls have to go far away places and stay in hostels or other residentials which are a hurdle for continuing education. Therefore, "the government should make every possible effort to start educational centres in areas which are easily accessible to all girls. As most of the teachers in the study wish to have separate school for girls, and as many studies have also supported this idea, "the government should establish separate schools for girls to promote enrollment as well as retaining them in schools". Further, the parents also have to pay much attention to educating their daughters equally regardless of their number. They should not force them into marriage until they become self-reliant. To realize this people in general and parents in particular have become aware of the importance of self-sustainability of girls and need of parental support to them. "The government and all those concerned with girl children should do everything possible to make girls self-dependent by creating opportunities of employment. Regarding respondents' opinion pertaining to their girl child's social participation, many of the respondents do not favour the participation of girls in both local and out-station competitions and in dance and music. So, there is a need to create awareness among respondents about the importance of sports and games for both physical and psychological development of girls. It is commonly observed the participation of girls in competition of sports and games at various levels is very moderate. So, "the government has to set up necessary supportive arrangements for encouraging the participation of girls in sports and games competitions".

Dance and music are rich sources of cultural transmission from one generation to another. They are precious parts of an heritage. If parents do not encourage their girls to learn them, they deny them a valuable opportunity to understand the richness of our culture. Further, there are several opportunities for both girls and boys in this field of fine arts as many media channels of communication, are available and there is a growing demand for talented persons. "Parents have to take the initiative and encourage their children to undergo training in dance and music. And the government for its part should set up schools of dance and music where training is given free of cost or at least at moderate fees".

Many parents do not favour their daughters having friends of opposite sex. They also do not think it necessary to consider the girl's opinion while finding a bridegroom for her. But this narrow-mindedness does great harm rather than good to the all-round development of the girl child. Girls expect to be understood and transited and given opportunities in decision-making. Therefore, parents of girl child must be friendly with them and give enough scope to their children to express and share their views. This attitude endears the parents to their children and helps them to become self-reliant as well as respondents. In this competitive world, the girl child has to acquire many skills for survival and find suitable employment. So "Parents have to provide enough support to their girl children to enrich their skills as generally they do to their sons. Further, outgrowing their prejudices regarding certain kinds of jobs for girls, they should help them to take in their stride any respectable job that comes their way and live with honour and dignity. Many respondents are anguished over increasing female foeticide. Strict legal implementation of laws against this crime must. More important is to change the widely prevalent attitudes against the birth of a girl child. There is no justification in religion for this attitude. Outmolded convention and beliefs have to be given up unable parents and people become so sensitized as to accept all children, girl or boy, gracefully and as gifts of God. No law or fear of penalty can arrest crimes of foeticide.

Economic independence of women is of very important for their empowerment as economic dependence of women on men is one of the important contributing factors for violence on women. In the present study it is found that many of the respondents, despite being teachers and parents, are not willing to give a share in property to their girl child, inspite of the government enacting of property rights for daughters equally with sons. Hence, there is much need to sensitize the respondents in this issue. Further, efforts should be made for the implementation of various legislations pertaining to property rights to facilitate girl child development and protect her rights. This enhances the economic independence of women. For the implementation and monitoring of laws/ programmes for the protection and welfare of the girl child, there is a need to set up appropriate mechanisms which are community based and recognized by panchayat raj institutions, self-help groups, other local bodies, etc.

Intensive measures have to be taken to control girl child abuse, violence, neglect and all evils on the girl children in society which have to be curbed immediately. As one looks at the various mass media, the television in particular, one suspects that many TV channels tend to dwell elaborately on instances of atrocities and violence against girls and women for their sensational value rather than as occasion to educate the human and ethical sustainabilities of the viewers and warn people of the consequence. The mass media have an enormous hold on the viewers' imagination. Most people tend to view uncritically what they see on the screen. And they are hardly aware that what they see unconscious feeds their pugnacious impulses. Therefore, the mass visual media, while exposing the atrocities, present them in the right perspective rather than for their sensational and titillating value. The media can and has to play an important role in bringing about a change in the mind-set of people by disseminating various and meaningful messages on factors responsible for girl child discrimination. Youth clubs, schools, colleges may be encouraged to participate in advocacy programmes against violence of the girl child through cultural programmes, capacity building, workshops, street theatre, story-telling, songs, posters and slogans, role play, etc.

Values determine attitudes and behaviour and so value-oriented education for the upcoming generations has to be introduced through schools to bring about attitudinal change which will facilitate gender equality.

Social Work Intervention

Despite almost five decades of planning constitutional commitments, legislations and programmes introduced to empower girls and promote their education, gender discrimination still prevails in our society. Hence, it is necessary to adopt a concerted effort to strengthen the resources of poor families in order to ensure them to fulfill the requirement of the girl child for promoting her education, health, nutritional care, etc.

The complexity of interrelationships of factors such as social, political, cultural, psychological, economical and physical and others call for the need of intervention by professional social workers. Social work intervention relating to the girl child issues is crucial and essential.

The social worker by using the methods of social work like case work, group work, community organization, social action, social work research utilizing the skills and techniques of social work can help people and victims of girl child abuse or discrimination to improve their situation.

The social worker can play different roles like educator, motivator, mediator, advocate counsellor, etc., to make people develop an egalitarian outlook regarding gender by utilizing available resources from governmental and non-governmental organizations.

The major goals of social work intervention with teachers are threefold–Ameliorate, preventive and promotional or developmental. Promotional or developmental help to the teachers enables them to enhance gender egalitarian attitudes /relationships, so that they can guide their students to understand the problems and thus sensitize them to the girl child's problems, eliminate false beliefs and influences which cause gender discrimination. Further, the social worker can make use of teachers as agents/instruments to promote gender sensitization among the public.

The social workers with the help of various non-governmental organizations may involve the teachers in group discussions to exchange ideas and expertise with the group members. Such exercises will help them to understand the girl child's situation and may facilitate them to evolve suitable strategies for the development of the girl child. In the same fashion, the social worker can form youth groups, self-help groups, etc., to help the government in organizing and implementing welfare activities for girl child.

The mass media are the best mode to spread information especially among illiterates. Social workers, by using the community organization method, organize film shows, exhibitions on the problems of the girl child in schools and in community. The social worker can organize awareness generation camps on issues relating to the girl child at the local level i.e., in various slums and villages to educate the community people about the need of reducing gender discrimination by removing the barriers of development of the girl child. Thus, the social worker can create awareness among teachers and public and help them to change their attitudes towards the girl child for the better.

The foregoing study has focused on the attitudes of teachers who are also parents regarding the girl child, their understanding and responses to the various issues that confront the girl child in our society. As they all live out function in Tirupati also expanding urban set-up which is on the way to become a cosmopolitan place, they are exposed to currents of new and fresher ideas on all issues of life. One would have expected from them as teachers and parents are enlighted approach to all the problems of the girl child. But the findings of the study show that there is not even near unanimity in their view. There are among the respondents who are enlightened as well as those whose attitudes are uncertain and ambiguous.

But, it is necessary to remember that the issues of the girl child in question concern all, not any one group or community or institution or government. Restoring to the girl child her rightful place and strains at home and in society is a collective responsibility. It means that individuals (parents, members of family, teachers, etc.), groups and communities have to endeavour together continuously and for long to achieve that goal. Because beliefs and attitudes regarding the girl child which have been hardened over centuries, cannot be dramatically changed overnight. No miracle can be expected. Steady, conscientious and continuous.

Attitudinal change can come only gradually, effort is necessary. Government may enact laws, initiate programmes of reform and provide the funds necessary from time to time. But they will not be worth the paper they are written on, if they are not implemented in letter and spirit. The tardy progress made in India over the years despite laws and programmes to protect the girl child's rights is proof enough for it. Effects to change outmoded attitudes, beliefs, customs and practices have to begin at home with parents and elderly members of the family. The school, which is in a sense, an extension of the family, and teachers there have to continue and strengthen what is begun at home. These two agencies—parents and teachers—can contribute significantly and enduringly to shaping the minds and hearts of children (boys and girls), and to help the girl child to acquire self-confidence and self-respect. What is begun at home and school can be and has to be extended further by other educational agencies. If parents and teachers have to deliver the goods to their children and pupils, they have to be educated. In their own they have to educate the measures without wasting for others. Education and learning is a never-ending process of growth of the mind and spirit. The efforts of government and non-governmental agencies to protect the girl child would been fruit, of the process of attitudinal change has already begun at home and school. Further and extensive research on the attitudes of parent-teacher towards the girl child and the various complex issues raised by the problems is necessary. The present study is only a modest beginning in that direction.

References

Agarwal, Shanta, (2006), "The Girl Child and her Education", Social Welfare, Vol. 53, No. 6, p. 27.

Alam, M. Sanjeer, (2007), "Interrogating Gendered Inequality in Educational Attainment in India", Social Change Vol. 37, No. 4, pp.153-179.

Aley, V.A., (2008), "Burnout and Anger in Teachers and Parents–Implications for Child Development", Indian Journal of Psychological Counselling, Vol. 16, pp. 11-18.

Ali, Jyothi, (2008), "Alarming Rise of Violence against Women: A View from Madhya Pradesh", Women's Link, Vol. 14, No. 2, pp.12-17.

Anand, Sarita, (2006), "Evaluating Campaigns against Female Foeticide", Social Welfare, Vol. 51, No. 11, pp. 19-24.

Andal Damodaran, (1999), "The Girl Child and You". Kodai Kanal, Mother Teresa Women's University News, Vol. 37 No. 15, pp. 15-17.

Anuradha, K., (2008), "Promoting Social Competency and Self-Perception in Children with Conduct Problems – A Social Group Work Approach", Contemporary Social Work, Vol. 11, No. 1, pp. 23-37.

Archinald, Andrea-Bastiani, Graber Julia A. and Brooks-Gunn, Jeanne, (1999), "Associations among parent adolescent relationships, parental growth, dieting and body image in young adolescent girl : A short-term longitudinal study", Journal of Research on Adolescence, Vol. 9, No. 4, pp. 395-415.

Asha Bajpai, (2007), "Who is a child?" available at www. infochange india.org.

Asha Bajpai, (2002), "Status of Children" available at www.infochangindia.org.

Asian Age, (2008), "Survey on Sex Ratio", 24-07-2008.

Attitudes, parental attitude towards the girl child, (2008), available at http://www.balika.org.

Bagchi J, Guha J. and Sangupta P., (2000), "The Girl Child Some Statistics", Loved and Unloved, Delhi, Stree Publications, pp.87-127.

Bahuguna, N.J., (2006), "New Tracks for Platform Children", Social Welfare, Vol. 53, No. 2, pp. 16-17.

Balingar, V.P., (1999), "Mother and Girl Child—Reconstructing Attitudes", New Delhi, Vedam Books, pp. 32-37.

Barbara Bruns, Alian Mingat and Ramahatra Rakotomalala, (2003), "Achieving Universal Primary Education by 2015 : A Chance for Every Child", Washington DC, The World Bank, pp. 23-29.

Barbara, A.M., and Theres, D., (1999), "Parental influences on toddlers injury-risk behaviours: Are sons and daughters socialized differently?" Journal of Applied Developmental Psychology, Vol. 20, No. 2, pp. 272-251.

Bhargava, Deepati, (1989), "Smriti—A Sociological Analysis", Jaipur, Rawat Publications, pp. 41-48.

Bhogle Shalini, (1999), "Child Rearing Practice and Bahaviour Development of Girl Child", Indian Journal of Social Work, Vol. 52, No. 1, pp. 61-69.

Bielawska-Batorowicz, Eleonosa, (1996), "Do mothers and fathers perceive their infants differently", Journal of Reproductive and Infant Psychology, Vol. 14, No. 4, pp. 277-292.

Bishoyi, Kedarnath, (2003), "Plight of Child Labour", New Delhi, Discovery Publishing House, pp. 48-50.

Campaign Against Child Labour, (2004-05), available at http://www.caclindia.org.

Campaign against child labour girl child labour years, (2003-2004), available at http://www.savegirllchild.org.

Carine and Janssens, (1998), "Maternal Influences on Daughter's Gender Role Attitudes", Journal of Sex Roles, Vol. 38, No. 3, pp. 171-186.

Census, (2001), Socio-cultural tables available at http://www.censusindia.com.

Centre for Social Research, (2007), "A Study on Child Marriage in India: Situational Analysis in Three States", Study Summary Report, New Delhi.

Chatterjee, Jyotsna, (2006), "Promoting Girl Child Friendly Society", available at http://grandhismriti.nic.

Chaudhury Paul D., "Girl Child and Gender Bias", Social Change, Vol. 25, No. 2 & 3, pp. 84-93.

Chaudhury, Paul, (1995), "Girl Child and Gender Bias", Social Change, Vol. 25, Nos. 2 & 3, pp. 84-93.

Child Labour. Impulse NGO Network, Shillong, Megalaya, available at, http://www.nrcw.org.

Child Protection and Rights, (2007), United Nations Convention on the Rights of the Child (UNCRC) available at www. childl ineindia.org.in

Chowdhury Leni, (2005), "Our Little Girl", available at http://www.sabrang.com

Chowdhury, A.R., (2006), "Cross Border Trafficking: The Indo Bangladesh Scenario", Social Welfare, Vol. 53, No. 2, pp. 32-33.

Chugh, Sunita, (2005), "Schooling for the urban poor : Insights from a slum study", Social Change, Vol. 35, No. 1, pp. 1-12.

Corson, D., (1993), Language, minority education and gender: Linking social justice and power Clevedon, UK: Multilingual matters, pp.18-35.

Das, N.C., (2008), "Need for Health Education in The 21st Century with special reference to Reproductive Health of Adolescents", Journal of Community Guidance and Research, Vol. 25, No. 2, pp. 185-191.

Das, Nimaicharan, (2007), "Counselling Service for Adolescents", Journal of Community Guidance and Research, Vol. 24, No. 1, pp. 9-14.

Das, Sibabrata, (2008), "Childhood Under nutrition: A Comparative Analysis of Scheduled Tribes and others in the mid-Indian Tribal Region", Social Change, Vol. 38, No. 1, pp. 64-83.

Dasgupta and Sarkar, (2008), "Menstrual Hygiene : How Hygienic is the adolescent girls?", Indian Journal of Community Medicine, Kolkata, Vol. 33, No. 4, pp. 77-80.

Dass, C.R., (2005), "Girl Child – Her Rights and Plights", in: Girl Child and Human Rights, eds., Chaudhury and Tripathy, New Delhi, Anmol Publications, pp. 91-98.

Deb, Sibnath, (1994), "Victimised Children of socio-economically disadvantaged families: A Calcutta based Study", 8th International Symposium on Victimology, Australian, Institute of Criminology, Adelaide, Australia, pp.21-26.

Deb, Sibnath, (2005), "Child Abuse and Neglect in a Metropolitan City: A Qualitative Study of Migrant Child Labour in South Kolkata", Social Change, Vol. 35, No. 3, pp. 56-67.

Deb, Sibnath, (2005), "Child Trafficking in South Asia: Dimensions, Roots, Facets and Interventions", Social Change, Vol. 35, No. 2, pp.143-155.

Deb, Sibnath and Senapati, Shishir, (1993), "Safety Needs of Abused Proleterian Bengalee Children", International and Inter-disciplinary Conference on Child Safety, University of Cape Town, South Africa.

Deepak Bishoyi, (2005), "Human Resource Development and Girl Child," in : Girl Child and Human Rights, "Eds, Chaudhury and Tripathy, New Delhi, Anmol Publications, pp. 48-60.

Desai, Murali, (1995), "Empowering the Family for Girl Child Development", Social Change, Vol. 25, Nos. 2 & 3, pp. 38-43.

Dhar, R., (2005), "Violence and Women", Social Change, Vol. 35, No. 4, pp.125-132.

Dubey Vimalesh Kumar, Dubey Akilesh Kumar and Singh, Harihar Prasad, (2008), "Impact of Information and Communication Technology on School Students", Journal of Communication Studies, Vol. 26, pp.45-55.

El-Gilang A.H., Badawi, K., (2005), "Menstrual Hygiene among adolescent School Girls in Mansoura, Egypt, Reproductive Health Matters, Vol. 13, pp. 147-152.

Gafoor, K.A., (2008), "Gender Equality Beliefs among Rural and Urban Boys and Girls", Journal of Community Guidance and Research, Vol. 25, No. 3, pp. 290-306.

Gangrade, K.D., (1995), "Social Development and the Girl Child", Social Change, Vol. 25, Nos. 2 & 3, pp. 70-82.

Geervani, P., (2000), "Empowerment of Women with special reference to Health", Workshop organized by National Commission for Women, S.V. University, Tirupati, 25th-26th November, 2000.

Ghai, Anita, (2006), "Education in a globalizing era : Implications for disabled girls", Social Change, Vol. 36, No. 3, pp. 161-176.

Ghosh, Shanti, (1995), "Integrated health of the girl child", Social Change, Vol. 25, Nos. 2 & 3, pp. 44-54.

Ghosh, Shanti, (1999), "Girl Child: A life time of deprivation and Discrimination", Indian Journal of Social Work, Vol. 52, No. 1, pp.21-27.

Girl Child in India, (2008), available at http://www.balika.org.

Girl Child in the Eleventh Five Year Plan, (2007-2012), Ministry of Women and Child Development, New Delhi, Government of India, pp. 1-38.

Gokhale, S.D., (1995), "Girl Child: Her Rights and Law", Social Change, 1995, Vol. 25, Nos. 2 & 3, pp. 116-118.

Goswami, S., (2006), "A Report on the Expectation of Children Expressed on Children's Day, November 14, 2003", Journal of Psychological Counselling, Vol. 15, pp. 16-27.

Goyal, Pratibha, (2005), "Child Labour in the Hosiery Industry of Ludhiana", Social Change, Vol. 35, No. 1, pp. 13-23.

International Institute for Population Sciences and ORC Macro, (2000), National Family Health Survey (NFHS-2), 1998-99: India, Mumbai, IIPS.

Jaya, S. and Jaya, N., (2006), "School as a Health Promoter among Adolescent Girls - A Feasibility Study", Journal of Psychological Counselling, Vol. 15, pp. 28-34.

Joshi, S.C., (2005), "A Comparative Study of Anxieties of the Adolescent Students of the Higher and Lower Economic Strata", Journal of Community Guidance and Research, Vol. 22, No. 3, pp. 299-306.

Kain, W.D., (1998), "Will sex determination lead to girl child elimination", Journal of Family Planning Association of India, Panchakula-Haryana Branch, Vol. 26, Nos. 3-5.

Kamo, Yoshinori, Warner-Rebecca, (1997), "The effect of children's sex on parent's gender role attitudes: An extension using Japanese Data", Journal of Comparative Family Studies, Vol. 28, No. 3, pp. 204-219.

Kanakadurga, (2003), "Reproductive Health among Adolescent and Young Girls: Issues of Concern", Contemporary Social Work, Vol.20, pp. 61-65.

Kanitkar, Tara, (1988), "Aspirations of Decision-makers for the Education of Girls, Bihar, 1980-81", Indian Journal of Social Work, Vol. 49, No. 2, pp. 163-177.

Karely, G.N., (2005), "Integrated Approach to Rural Development, Policies, Programmes and Strategies", New Delhi, Concept Publish Company, p. 63.

Karkal, (1999), "Invisibility of the Girl Child in India", Indian Journal of Social Work, Vol. 52, No. 1, pp. 5-12.

Kaur, Manmeet, (1993), "Female Foeticide – A Socio Logical Perspective, The Journal of Family Welfare, Vol. 39, No. 1, pp. 40-43.

Kaur, Manmeet, (2006), "Protecting Girl Child: Challenges", Promoting Girl Child Friendly Society, chandigarh, C.Y.P. Asia Centre.

Khan, W.H., (2004), "Barriers to Girls' Education" available at http://www.indiatogether.

Leelamma, Devasia and Devasia, (1991), "Girl Child in India", New Delhi, Ashish Publishing House.

Limage, Sandhya, (2008), "The Inner World of Adolescent Girls with Hearing Impairment : Two Case Studies", Indian Journal of Gender Studies, Vol. 15, No. 2, pp. 387-406.

Loya Mainsnam, (2009), "Girls and Gender Discrimination" available at http://www.e-pao.net.

Mahajan, V. and Sharma, D., (2006), "Are Adolescents at Mental Health Risk in Single Parent Families?", The Indian Journal of Social Work, Vol. 67, No. 4, pp. 353-369.

Maheswari, K.U., (2005), "Effectiveness of Nutrition Education Programme on the Knowledge Scores of Adolescent School Girls", Journal of Communication Studies, Vol. 23, No. 7, pp. 65-69.

Majumdar, Swapna, (2006), "Festival for Girls", Social Welfare, Vol. 52, No.3, pp. 16-17.

Manjula, B.C., (2008), "Deserted Women breaking their Silence", Women's Link, Vol. 14, No. 2, pp. 25-28.

Mathew, Susy, (2000), "Women's Human Rights", available at http://jainsamaj.org/literature/women.

Mathur, G. and Verma, R., (2007), "Attitude of Adolescents towards Violence and Aggression depicted in Movies", Journal of Community Guidance and Research, Vol. 24, No. 1, pp. 15-20.

Ministry of Health and Family Welfare available at http://www.mhfw.in.

Ministry of Human Resource Development, National Commission for Co-operation with UNESCO, (2001), "Women teachers in rural India", available at http://nrcw.nic.in.

Ministry of Planning, Bangladesh, (2003), "Fifth Five-Year Plan (1997-2002)". Journal of Public Administration, p. 15.

Mishra, Jayasree, (2000), "The Girl Child in a Scavenging Community" New Delhi, Manak Publications, pp. 21-31.

Misra, R.N., (2003), "Child Labour in Hazardous Sectors", New Delhi, Discovery Publishing House, pp. 76-82.

Mita Bhadra, (1999), "Introduction" in Girl Child in Indian Society, Mita Bhadra (Ed)), New Delhi, Rawat Publications, pp. 18-21.

Mittal, L.N., (1996), "Child Prostitution and Sex Tourism", Central Social Welfare Board, Social Welfare, Vol. 43, No. 5, pp. 23-26.

Mohanthy, P.C., (2005), "Gender Bias—A Sociological Approach. available at http://www.orissa.gov.in.

Mohanty, Ranjan, (2003), "Freeing the Girl Child Labour year", Campaign Against Child Labour (CACL), available at http://www.savegirlchild.org.

Mohsini, S.R., (1991), "The Status and Education of the Girl Child" in Devasia and Devasia (Eds.) Girl Child in India, New Delhi, Ashish Publishing House, pp. 85-94.

Mondal, N.I., Hossain, K.M. and Ali, K.M., (2006), "Women's Status in Bangladesh", The Indian Journal of Social Work, Vol. 67, No. 4, pp.341-351.

Mukherjee, (1991), "The Girl Child in India", Indian Journal of Paediatrics, Vol. 58, No. 3, pp. 301-303.

Mukherjee, Protap and Saraswathi, L.R., (2005), "Women's Empowerment and Gender Preferences for Children: A Study of Four Metropolitan Cities in India", available at www.isical.ac.in/nwemp.

Mukhopadhyay Ashim, (1997), "Girl Child in Three Indian States", Economic and Political Weekly, June p. 1379.

My Name if Today, (2002), "Anti-trafficking Network, NGO", Vol. 10, pp. 48-52.

Naachimuthu, K.P. and Rekha, R.N., (2008), "A Study on Guidance Needs of School-going Adolescents", Indian Journal of Psychological Counselling, Vol. 16, pp. 1-10.

Nagda, B.L., (2006), "Elimination of Female Children", Social Welfare, Vol.53, No. 1, pp. 19-24.

Nair, M.K.C. and Pejaver, R.K., (2001), "Child Welfare", available at http://nrcw.nic.in.

National Commission for Women, (1997), available at http://www.ncw.in.

National Crime Record Bureau, (2006-2007), "Crimes against children, Human Trafficking", available at http://ncrbinic.in.

National Institute of Nutrition, (2003), "Nutrition Prevalence of Micro-nutrient deficiencies", available at http://nrcw.nic.in.

National Institute of Public Co-operation and Child development, (2004), "Growth and Development" available at http://nrcw.nic.in.

National Policy on Education, (1986), Ministry of Human Resource Development, Government of India, pp. 1-20.

National Resource Centre for Women, (2003), "Girl Child Discrimination" available at http://www.nrcw.nic.in.

National Sample Survey Organization, (1997), Table 4.3.1, EPW, Vol. 32, Nos. 1 & 4.

Nayar, U.S., (1999), "Labour of the Indian Girl Child. Multi-curse, Multi-abuse and Multi-Neglect, Indian Journal of Social Work, Vol. 52, No. 1, pp. 37-47.

NCERT, (2005), "National Curriculum Framework, 2005: Position Paper on Gender Issues in Education, New Delhi.

Ninapuri, (1998), "The Girl Child in India", The Journal of Family Welfare, Vol. 44, No. 3, pp. 1-7.

Pal, R.M., (1997), "Rights of the girl child as Human Rights", Women's Link, pp. 7-12.

Pandey R. and Prasad R.E., (2006), "Effect of Child to Parent Communication Technique: A Comparative Study", Journal of Communication Studies, Vol. 24, pp. 17-23.

Parikh, D., (2006), "The Effect of Learning Disability on Self-esteem and Peer Relations", Journal of Psychological Consellling, Vol. 15, pp.10-15.

Pasayat C., (2005), "Girl Child Workers in our Society" in: Girl Child and Human Rights, eds. Chaudhury D. and Tripathy S.N., New Delhi, Anmol Publications pp. 61-76.

Pasayat, C., (2000), "Need of educating Tribal Children in Orissa" in Tripathy (ed.), Glimpses on Tribal development, Discovery Publishing House, New Delhi, pp. 29-42.

Patel, (1998), "Primary Schooling and the Girl Child in Rural Areas", Women's Link, Vol. 4, No. 4, pp. 13-16.

Patil, K., (2006), "Child Abuse, Neglect and Violence and its Impact on their Future", Indian Journal of Psychological Counselling, Vol. 15, pp. 1-9.

Philip, Tomy and Parashar, Nidhi, (2006), "Family Satisfaction and Subjective Well being of Adolescent Children having parents with schizophrenia", Perspectives in Social Work, Vol. 21, No. 2, pp.12-20.

Plan of Action for Implementing World Declaration on Survival, Protection and Development of Children, (1990), World Summit for Children, United Nations, New York, UNICEF, New York, pp. 1-2.

Pradhan P. Mohanty N. and Achary, A.K., (2005), Girls Education Commitment or Neglect? In Girl Child and Human Rights, eds. Debadutta and Tripathy, New Delhi, Anmol Publications, pp. 38-47.

Prakash, B., (2007), "Demography-adolescents in India", Endeavour, Vol.1, No. 1, p. 23.

Priyadarshini, T. and Tiwari Garim, (2006), "2005 Amendment of Hindu Succession Act recognition of women's property rights?" Perspectives in Social Work, Vol. 21, No. 1, pp. 9-15.

Pumphi, (2005), "World Health Organization Report, 2003". Assistant Director General, WHO, Geneva, qut in "Neglect is killing more baby girls than boys", Women's Link, Vol. 11, No. 3, p. 51.

Punalekar, S.P., (1995), "Culture, Political Economy and Gender Marginalization : A Case of Girl Child in India, Social Change, Vol. 25, Nos. 2 & 3, pp. 55-68.

Quraishi, (1991), "Factor analysis of Teachers Attitudes towards various Groups and Practices", Journal of Psychological Research, Vol. 35, No. 1, pp. 24-27.

Raj, Bhanti, (1995), "The Tribal Girl in Rajasthan", Social Change, Vol. 25, No. 2 & 3, pp. 203-206.

Ranjan, Y., (2008), "Child Labour have we to feigh ignorance?" Available at http://www.e-pao.net.

Ranjana Kumari, (2006), "Female Infanticide and Foeticide: The Declining Sex Ratio", New Delhi, Centre for Social Research, pp.1-22.

Rao, D.T. and Misra, R.N., (2005), "Problems of Girl Child Labour in Small Industries: A Study" in Girl Child and Human Rights, eds., Chaudhury, D. and Tripathy, S.N., New Delhi, Anmol Publications, pp. 99-109.

Rekha, D., (1995), "Status of Tribal Girl Child", Social Change, Vol. 25, No. 2 & 3, pp. 207-216.

Renu, A., (2007), "Mainstreaming disability into the child rights agenda", available at http://infochangeindia.org/.

Roul, Sushanta Kumar and Sahoo, Rudra Narayan, (2005), "Dropout among girls at Elementary level: A Study of Casual Factors", Journal of Community Guidance and Research, Vol. 22, No. 3, pp.292-298.

Ruiselova, Zdena, (1998), "Relationships with parents and teachers in connection with pubertal maturation timing in girls". Studia-Psychologica, Vol. 40, No. 4, pp. 277-281.

Saini, Saritha, (2007), "Psychological Problems of Adolescent Children", Journal of Community Guidance and Research, Vol. 24, No. 3, pp.290-297.

Santha, Sinha, (2000), "Impact of Girl Child's Enrollment on work sharing and distribution pattern in families", available at http://www.mvfindia.com.

Sarada, S. and Lakshmi, P., (2008), "Violence against Women – Need for a Social Change", Women's Link, Vol. 14, No. 2, pp. 29-35.

Saraswat, R., (2006), "Child Marriage: A Social Evil", Social Welfare, Vol.53, No. 1, pp. 15-16.

Save the Children, (2006), Protection, Education, HIV and AIDS Emergencies, available at http://www.savethechildren.in/india.

Sen, Amartya and Dreze, Jean, (1995), "India : Economic Development and Social Opportunities", Oxford University Press, pp. 55-59.

Seventh All India Education Survey, (2002), available at http://education.nic.in.

Sharma Shubhangna, (2007a), "Home based Intervention for Improvement of Socio-Emotional Competencies in Children", Indian Council of Agricultural Research available at http://hillagric.ernet.in.

Sharma Subhangana, (2007d), "Empowerment of rural girl child for quality life "Indian Councial of Agricultural Research, New Delhi, available at : http://www.hillangric.ernet.in.

Sharma Subhangna, (2007b), "Comprehensive Child care through farm Creche-Intervention for Optimum Developmental Outcome of young children", Indian Council of Agricultural Research, New Delhi available at http://hillagric.ernet.in.

Sharma Subhangna, (2007c), "Assessment of Health Status of Adolescent Girls belonging to Gaddi Tribes of Himachal Pradesh, 2002-2004, available at http://hillangric-ernet.in.

Sharma, Adarsh, (1995), "Socio-cultural Practices threatening the girl child", Social Change, Vol. 25, Nos. 2 & 3, pp. 94-105.

Sharma, Neerja, (1996), "Identity of the Adolescent Girl", New Delhi, Discovery Publishing House, pp.

Sharma, Pushpa and Chikara, Sudha and Krishna, (1997), "Nutrition of Girl Child: A Positive Change", Journal of Family planning Association of India, Vol. , No. , pp. 5 & 6.

Sharma, Ramakant, (2006), "Changing Age at Marriage", Social Welfare, Vol. 53, No. 1, pp. 17-18.

Shinde, Pratibha, (2007), "Malnutrition amongst Maharashtra's Tribals: How bad is it?" available at Info Change News and Features, infochangeindia.org.

Shukla, C.K. and Ali, S., (2006), "Child Labour: Socio-Economic Dimensions", New Delhi, Sarup and Sons, pp. 52-59.

Silverstein, Brett, Clauson, Joanne: Perdue, Lauren: Carpman, Shari and Cimarolli: Verena, (1998), "The Association between female college student's reports of depression and their perceptions of parental attitudes regarding gender". Journal of Applied Social Psychology, Vol. 28 No. 6, pp. 537-549.

Singhe, Mohan and Kazi, A.S., (2006), "Perceived parental attitudes to wards the blind children", Perspectives in Social Work, Vol. 21, No. 1, pp. 38-41.

Sisodia, Yatindra Singh, (2003), "Girl's Literacy in Rural India", Jaipur, Rawat Publications, pp. 198-205.

Smile Foundation, (2003), "Gender Discrimination", available at http://www.smilefoundationindia.org.

Sorta, Bilajac, I., (2004), "Indian Bioethics: The issue of Female Foeticide and Infanticide, A sikh perspective, Ethecs and politics 2004, available at http://www.units.it/etica/2004/sortabilajac.htm.

Srivastava, Nilima, (2006), "Women and Higher Education: Need and Benefit", Journal of Social Welfare, Vol. 53, No. 6, pp. 28-29.

Sudha, S. and Rajan, I.S., (2003), "Persistent Daughter Disadvantage: What do Estimated Sex Ratio at birth and Sex ratio of Child Mortality, risk reveal?", Economic and Political Weekly, Vol. 38, No. 41, pp. 11-17.

Sultana, S.A. and Velayuthan, S.K., (2006), "Quality in Early Childhood Care and Education—Are we really concerned?", Social Welfare, Vol. 53, No. 6, pp. 30-33.

Swarnalatha, A. and Vasantha, K., (2007), "Attitudes, Knowledge and Beliefs of Adolescent Girls on Reproductive Health", Journal of Community Guidance and Research, Vol. 24, No. 3, pp.373-381.

Swarr, Amy, E., Richards, Maryse, H., (1996), "Longitudinal effects of adolescent girls", Pubertal Development, Practices of Pubertal Timing and Parental Relations on eating problems", Journal of Development Psychology, Vol. 34, No. 4, pp. 636-646.

Talukdar, N.N. and Talukdar, M.C., (2008), "Adjustment Problems of Adolescent Students", Journal of Community Guidance and Research, Vol. 25, No. 3, pp. 267-271.

The Hindu, (2001), "Destroyed Childhood" available at http://www.hinduonnet.com.

The Tribune, (1995), "Free Education for Girls in HImachal Pradesh", July 3, 1995.

Tilaye, K. and Bendru, K., (2006), "Girl's Performance in Mathematics in Upper Primary Schools of Addis Ababa", Indian Journal of Gender Studies, Vol. 13, No. 3, pp. 401-424.

Tripathy and Chaudhury, (2005), "Denial of Rights of Girl Child: A Violation of Human Rights" in Girl Child and Human Rights, Eds by Chaudhury and Tripahy, New Delhi, Anmol Publications, pp. 1-6.

Tripathy, S., (2005), "Politico-Morality of Human Rights: A Vision of Indian Gil Child" in Girl Child Human Rights, Eds. Chaudhury, D. and Tripathy, New Delhi, Anmol Publishers. pp. 77-82.

Tripathy, S.N., (2004), "Tribal Migration", New Delhi, Sonali Publications, p. 25-40.

Tripathy, S.N. and Pradhan, Premananda, (2003), "Girl Child in India", New Delhi, Discovery Publishing House, pp. 13-15.

UNICEF, (1990), "Growing up as a Girl", Children and Women in India, A Situation Analysis, New Delhi.

UNICEF, (1991), "The Girl Child in India-SAARC year of the girl child, New Delhi, India, Country Office, UNICEF.

UNICEF, (2004), "Child marriage is a gross violation of all categories of Child rights", available at: http://infochangeindia.org.

Vandana, P., (1997), "Health and Nutrition of the Girl Child", Women's Link, pp. 13-16.

Verma, M.M. and Verma, Bhavana, (2007), "Women's Health: Role of Social Work", Contemporary Social Work, Vol. 1, pp. 77-92.

Vidyasagar, K., (2007), "Educational Challenges and the Role of Teachers in Andhra Pradesh: A case for Institutional Initiatives", Journal of Social and Economic Development, Vol. 9, No. 2, pp. 178-198.

Vidyasagar, K., (2007), "Educational Inequality and Teacher Performance in Andhra Pradesh: Challenges Ahead", Social Change, Vol. 37, No. 1, pp. 98-124.

Wadsworth, M., E.J., (1996), "Social and Historical Influences on Parent-Child Relations in Mid Life", Psychological Research, Vol. 84, No. 30, pp.169-212.

Women Studies Development Centre, (2007), "Assessment of Attitudinal Difference towards girl child in selected districts of North India" available at http://www.du.ac.in/wsdc.girlchild.

World Bank Report, (1996), "Engendering Development through Gender Equality in Rights Resources and Voice", World Bank Policy Research Report, New York, Oxford University Press, available at http://www.worldbank.org.

World Declaration on Survival, Protection and Development of Children, (1990), World Summit for Children, United Nations, New York, UNICEF, p. 2.

Yadav, Aradhana, (2006), "Little Adults in the World of Work", Social Action, Vol. 56, pp. 65-78.

Yadav, V.S., Anjumala, T.N. and Gaonkar, V., (2005), "A Critical Analysis of Identity Style and Adjustment among College Students", Journal of Community Guidance and Research, Vol. 22, No. 2, pp.144-156.

Appendix

Interview Schedule

Parents Opinion Towards Girl Child–A Study Amongst School Teachers In Tirupati

Part–I

The Socio-Economic Demographic Information of the Respondents

1. Name of the Respondent:
2. Name of the School and Address:
3. Age of the respondents
   (1) Upto 30 years (2) 30-40 years
   (3) 40-50 years (4) Above 50 years
4. Sex of the Respondent
   (1) Male (2) Female
5. Religion
   (1) Hindu (2) Muslim
   (3) Christian (4) Any other specify
6. Caste
   (1) Forward Caste (2) Other Backward Castes
   (3) Scheduled Castes (4) Scheduled Tribes
7. Marital Status
   (1) Married (2) Divorced/separated
   (3) Widow/Widower (4) Unmarried

8. Educational Qualifications
   (1) Upto Intermediate (2) Graduation
   (3) Post-graduation (4) Ph.D
9. The training undergone
   (1) Teacher training (2) B.Ed.
   (3) M.Ed. (4) Technical training
   (5) B.P.Ed. etc.
10. Type of family
   (1) Joint (2) Nuclear
11. Family Constellation

Name	*Relationship*	*Education*	*Occupation*	*Monthly Income*	*Remarks*

12. School in which the respondent is working
   (1) Government school (2) Government aided school
   (3) Private school (4) Any other specify
13. Monthly income of the respondent
   (1) Upto Rs. 3,000 (2) Rs. 3,001 to 6,000
   (3) Rs. 6,001 to 9,000 (4) Rs. 9,001 to 12,000
   (5) Rs. 12,001 and above
14. What are the other sources of income
   (1) No other sources (Other than spouse)
   (2) House rent
   (3) Agriculture and allied
   (4) Interests and returns on saving, etc.
   (5) Business
   (6) Any other specify

15. Is there any saving by you?
    (1) Yes (2) No
16. If Yes, savings per month
    (1) Less than Rs. 1000 (2) Rs. 1001 to 2000
    (3) Rs. 2001 and above (4) Not applicable
17. Are your economic sources enough to meet your essential needs
    (1) No (2) Partly
    (3) Completely
18. If no, how do you manage?
    (1) By taking loans from banks & office
    (2) By taking loans from money-lenders
    (3) By taking loans from relatives and friends
    (4) Using savings etc.,
    (5) Not applicable
19. For what purpose you have taken loans
    (1) Son's education, employment, business
    (2) Daughter's education, employment and business
    (4) Daughter's Marriage
    (5) Health of the family
    (6) Any other specify
    (7) Not applicable
20. Duration of repayment of loans by the respondents
    (1) Monthly (2) Half yearly
    (3) Yearly (4) Whenever possible
    (5) Not applicable

PART–II

Information Regarding the Respondents' Opinion About their Girl Child's Education

	Strongly Agree	Agree	Dis-agree	Strongly Disagree
21. Education is very important for girls.				
22. Parents play important role to reduce school dropouts rate of girls under any circumstances.				
23. Minimum education like Inter, graduation is not enough for girls.				
24. High professional education like engineer-ing, medicine is necessary for girls.				
25. The govt. school education is not enough for girls.				
26. Even high donations can be invested on girls, school education.				
27. Even donations upto degree level can be invested on girls education.				
28. Donation can be invested on girls education for professional courses like engineering and medicine.				

	Strongly Agree	*Agree*	*Dis-agree*	*Strongly Disagree*
29. Outside the state, any amount for professional courses can be invested on girls.				
30. Private and best school education is necessary for girls also.				
31. Parents must help girls in their education at home.				
32. Tuitions must be arranged for girls also.				
33. Government provisions like reservation, free education etc., are necessary for girls.				
34. Girl children also need recreation and education which will be acquired through study tours to far away places and competitions for children.				

Opinion of the Respondents about Their Girl Child's Health and Nutritional Care

	Strongly Agree	*Agree*	*Dis-agree*	*Strongly Disagree*
35. Parents play an important role in girl child's health.				
36. Regular health check-ups are necessary for girl children.				

	Strongly Agree	Agree	Dis-agree	Strongly Disagree
37. Parents must identify and treat the health problems of girl children at an early stage.				
38. Home remedies are enough to treat girl childrens' health problems.				
39. Hospital treatment is a must to treat girls children's health problems.				
40. The girl child must be provided more nutritious and balanced diet regularly.				
41. Parents must provide salads & fruits to their girl children.				
42. Parents must give pocket money for girls to purchase eatables, etc.				

Opinion of the Respondents Regarding Their Girl Child's Social Participation

	Strongly Agree	Agree	Dis-agree	Strongly Disagree
43. Girl children also need to participate in sports.				
44. Girl children also need to participate in indoor games.				

	Strongly Agree	Agree	Dis-agree	Strongly Disagree
45. Girl children need training in fine arts like dance, music etc.				
46. Girl children need to participate in competitions in local.				
47. Girl children also need to participate in competitions of sports, fine arts, etc., which are conducted outside the station.				
48. There is no need for separate schools for girl children.				
49. Girl children must undergo training in martial arts for protection of themselves from any dangers.				
50. Training in housekeeping and other activities must be given girl children.				
51. Girl children must be provided training in marketing, purchasing, payments of electricity bills etc.,				
52. Marriage of girl children should be performed after attaining the required age (Female-21).				

	Strongly Agree	*Agree*	*Dis-agree*	*Strongly Disagree*
53. Girl children must be given property.				
54. Girl children must be given opportunity to select their life partners.				
55. Parents must give value to their girl child's ideas regarding dress, food, recreation etc.,				
56. Parents should not give dowry for their girl children				
57. Girl children can have friends for social interaction.				
58. Girl children can have friends of the opposite sex.				

Opinion of the Respondents about Their Girl Child's Psychological Development

	Strongly Agree	*Agree*	*Dis-agree*	*Strongly Disagree*
59. Developing good personality for girl child is important.				
60. Parent's can influence the girl child's personality.				
61. Parents must train their girl children to develop self-confidence and to manage crisis situations.				

	Strongly Agree	*Agree*	*Dis-agree*	*Strongly Disagree*
62. Parents must help girl children to develop self esteem.				
63. Parents must be friendly with their girl children for better understanding.				
64. Parents must give punishment to girl children when they are not studying.				
65. Parents must give punishment to girl children for their misbehaviour.				
66. Parents should not compel only girls to do household work.				

Opinion of the Respondents about Employment Support for Their Girl Child

	Strongly Agree	*Agree*	*Dis-agree*	*Strongly Disagree*
67. Girl children must be trained in jobs oriented courses only.				
68. Parents must invest large amounts of money to provide special training to their girl children for jobs.				
69. Parents must provide money as security for girl children to get jobs.				

		Strongly Agree	Agree	Dis-agree	Strongly Disagree
70.	Parents must send their girl children to far away places for doing jobs.				
71.	Parents must provide training to their girl children in teaching nursing, etc., only				
72.	I prefer jobs like conductor, driver, administrators, mechanics etc to my daughter (s).				
73.	I prefer jobs like touring jobs, marketing, etc., also to my daughter (s).				
74.	I prefer jobs like Doctor, Engineer, Lecturer etc., to my daughter(s).				

PART–III

Respondents' Opinion about Government Welfare Schemes for the Betterment of Girl Child

		Strongly Agree	Agree	Dis-agree	Strongly Disagree
75.	Free education for girls upto degree level is very beneficial for girl education				
76.	Balika samrakshna pathakam is very useful to balance sex ratio and prevent gender discrimination				
77.	The Kishore Balika scheme is encouraging employment skills, opportunities and health awareness of girl children.				
78.	Kishore Balika scheme is providing awareness of family life education to girl children.				
79.	Apni Beti Apna Desh Programme is very useful to rehabilitate the girls who are rescued from child labour and brothel homes.				
80.	Strict implementation of pre-natal diagnostic technique (Regulation, Prevention & Misuse) Act, 1994 helps in reducing female foeticide.				

81. Constitutional provision and human rights for girl child reduces gender discrimination.
82. National policy for children and legal enactments facilitate development of girl child.
83. The present welfare measures taken by government and non-governmental organizations are sufficient to improve the girl child status.

Index

A

Adolescent Gaddi Girls, 37

Andhra Pradesh, 4, 6, 7, 15, 77

Apni Beti Apna Desh, 19

Program, 122

Awareness Programs, 147

B

Balika Samridhi Yojna, 19

Bangladesh, 58

Brahmanical Law Givers, 42

Breastfeeding, 10

C

Cashew Processing, 17

Casteism, 17

CEDAW, 72

Centre for Women's Develop-ment Studies, 69

Child

Health and Education, 5

Child Labour, 7, 16, 17

Socio-Economic Problem, 58

Labour Protection and Registration Act, 19

Labourers, 7, 41

Marriage, 3, 4, 6, 24, 41, 42, 72

Abolition of-, 18

Marriage Restraint Act, (CMRA), 6, 14, 20, 147

Mortality Rate, 4

Prostitution, 15

Protection, 1

Rape, 14

Rights, 1

Sex Ratio, 5

Workers, 56

Children in Prostitution, 44

China, 43

Commercial Sex Workers, 16

Crimes against Children, 14

Crisis Management, 114

Customary Laws, 5

Customs, 1, 3

Customs and Rituals, 3

D

Dance and Music, 164
Data Collection, 80
Different Groups of Prostitutes, 16
 Caste-Based Brothels, 16
 Religious Prostitutes, 16
 Singing and Dancing Girls, 16
Disabled Girl Child, 45
Discrimination
 Against Girl Child, 24
 Of Girl Child, 3, 4
District
 Chittoor, (Andhra Pradesh), 76, 77
 Kangra and Chamba, 37
 Kurnool-Tirupati, 77
 Mayurbhanj, 30
Donations, 97
Dowry, 3
 Prohibition Act, 1961, 19, 147
 System, 5
Dropouts, 146
 Rates, 26

E

Economic
 And Cultural Patterns of Society, 44
 Information, 93
Economy, 8
Education, 7, 8
 For Girls, 25
 For Women, 26
 Infancy and Childhood, 30
Educational
 Backwardness of Women/Girls, 26
 Program, 45
 System in India, 59
Ethnic Practices, 1
Eve Teasing, 8

F

Family Planning Methods, 38
Female
 Foeticide, 5, 6, 12, 13, 46
  Causes, 12
 Foeticide and Infanticide, 19, 72
 Foeticide District in India, 12
 Infanticide, 6, 12, 13, 18
 Literacy, 5
 Mortality, 146
 Teachers, 8
Financial Management, 92
Five Year Plan (11th), 1, 72
Foeticide, 12, 13
Foeticide Cases, 14

G

Gaddi Tribes of Himachal Pradesh, 37
Gender Discrimination, 3, 4, 11, 17, 138
Girl
 Prostitutes, 16
 Prostitution, 16
Girl Child
 Abuse, 14
 Defined, 1
 Demographic Concept, 4

Discrimination, 40, 147
Education, 24, 54, 73, 74, 94, 97, 126, 127, 130, 153-154
Education-Employment Support, 24
Educational Status, 8
Employment, 138
Employment Support, 80, 159
Health or Nutrition, 155
Health, 31, 75, 76
Labour, 4, 72
  Causes or-, 17
  Force, 16
Labourers, 8, 17, 57
Legal Support, 18
Marriage, 43
Mortality, 4, 6
Parental Support, 61
Problems in India, 11
Psychological Development, 113, 158
Rights, 60
Social Participation, 135, 156-157
  In Sports/Games, 106
Socio-Economic Status, 152
Status, 73
Workers, `16
  Bidi/Cigar Rolling, 16
  Match Fire Works, 17
  Plantation, 16

Girl's
  Education, 28, 29
  Schooling, 27

Girls
  In Tribal Societies, 56
  Literacy, 28

Glass and Bangles Factories in Firozabad, 59
Government Welfare Schemes, 159-161
Gujarat, 45

H

Health
  Education, 39
  Problems, 103
HIV/AIDS, 11, 39
  Virus, 15
Houschold Economy, 73
Human
  Rights for Girl Child, 122, 123
  Trafficking, 14

I

Immoral Trafficking Prevention Act, 1929, 20
India's Primary Education, 9
Indian
  Council of Agriculture Research, (ICAR), 27
  Society, 23, 38
Industrialization, 17, 88
Infant
  And Child Mortality, 26
  Mortality Rate, 13
Infanticide Cases, 14
Infanticides, 13
Information, Communication and Technology, 52

Integrated Child Development Scheme (ICDS), 19, 20, 32
International
Conference on Population and Development, Cairo, 31
Instruments, 72
Labor Organization, (ILO), 16
Interview Schedule, 79
IPC Crimes, 14

J

Jammu and Kashmir, 57
Job Oriented
Courses, 117
Training, 116

K

Kasturba Gandhi Shiksha Yojna, 19
Kishori Balika Schemes, 122

L

Law Enforcement Methods, 16
Legal Measures by Govt. of India, 18-19
Liberty, 4, 5
Literacy Rate, 56
Rate in India, 25
Ludhiana Hosiery Industry, 41

M

Madhya Pradesh, 14
Maharashtra, 14
Major Findings, 148-152
Male
Child as SWOGOTRA, 3
Dominated Society 2, 73
Marital Status of Respondents, 88
Mass Media, 167
Match/Fire Works in Sivakashi, 59
Maternal Mortality Rate, 5
Migration, 26
Millennium Development Goals, 25
Ministry of Labour, 7
Women and Child Development, 20
Money Savings, 91
Muslim Community, 133, 134

N

National
Commission for Women (NCW), 15, 16
Crime Records Bureau (NCRB), 14
Plan of Action for Girl Child, 19
Policy for Child, 123, 124
Policy of Education, 19, 147
Non-Governmental Organizations (NGOs), 7, 29, 43, 46, 59, 69, 124
North East Indian States, 68

O

Occupational Stresses, 68

P

Palna Scheme, 19
Patriarchy, 1
PDTA (Pre-Natal Diagnostic Techniques Act), 1994, 12
Pornographic Magazines, 15
Private School Education for Girl Child, 99
Professional Courses, 97, 98
Prostitution, 14, 16, 17, 72
Prostitution, Selling Girls for-, 14
Purdah System, 25

R

Rajasthan, 45
Rajasthan-Tamil Nau, 6
Rajasthan-Uttar Pradesh, 6
Rape, 42
Rayalaseema Region, 76
Religious Beliefs, 1
Reproductive Health, 38
Rights of Girl Child, 4, 146

S

SAARC Region, 1
Salvation, 3
Sarva Shiksha Abhiyan, 20
Save the Children, 57
Scheduled Caste
    Children, 40
    Welfare, 69
Scheduled Castes/Tribes, (SC/ST), 56
    Girls, 56
Scheduled Tribes, 40
School
    Education for Girl Child, 96
    Enrolment and Dropouts, 4
    Lunch Program, 70
Selective Abortions, 13
Sex
    Determination, 12, 40
    Differentiation, 86
    Pre-Selection, 12
    Ratio in-, 6
        Gujarat, 6
        Haryana, 6
        Punjab, 6
Sexual
    Abuse, 15
    Harassment, 8
    Violence, 42
Social
    And Economic Justice, 58
    Development, 26
    Participation, 133
    Sanctions, 42
Socialization, 23
Socio-Economic Status, 3
South Asian Region, 1
Status of Girl Child in India, 23
Stree Dhan, 3

T

Teachers' Socio-Economic Profiles, 74
Tirumalai Hills, 77
Tirupati-Tirumalai Pilgrim Centre, 77
Torture Preventive Centre in India, 15
Trafficking, 44
    In Children, 43
    In South Asian Region, 44
Training in
    Crisis Management, 114
    Marketing, 109
Tribal
    Girls, 56
    Society, 69

U

Ultra Sonography, 12
UN
    Convention on Elimination of all Forms of Discrimination against Women (CEDAW), 18
    Convention on Rights of Child, 72

UNCRC (UN Convention on the Rights of Child), 1
UNICEF, 7, 15, 20, 43, 57
University Grants Commission (UGC), 30
Urbanization, 29
Uttar Pradesh, 45

V

Violation against Human Rights, 16
Vocational Training, 7

W

Welfare Schemes for Girls, 119
Women
    Reservation, 46
    Teachers, 30
Women's
    Education in India, 24
    Education, 30
    Empowerment, 28
    Participation-Higher Education, 30
    Status, 72
    Studies and Development Centre, 11
World
    Health Organization (WHO), 38, 43
    Summit for Children, 16